GATESHEAD

history & guide

GATESHEAD

history & guide

Alan Brazendale

TEMPUS

First published 2004

Tempus Publishing Ltd
The Mill, Brimscombe Port
Stroud, Gloucestershire GL5 2QG
www.tempus-publishing.com

British Library Cataloguing in Publication Data.
A catalogue record for this book is available from the British Library.

ISBN 0 7524 3207 9

Typesetting and origination by Tempus Publishing.
Printed in Great Britain

Contents

Foreword

I am delighted to have been asked to write this foreword, because I never realized until I read Alan's book quite what a rich and interesting history we share.

Of course there are accounts of the many familiar characters we know and their links with Gateshead – the likes of Geordie Ridley, Thomas Hepburn, Joseph Swan and great sporting champions of the past like Renforth and Clasper. But I was also pleased to find some of the lesser known characters – like Konni Zilliacus, one of Gateshead's most outspoken MPs. He managed to get expelled from the Labour Party and was refused entry to both the Soviet Union and the USA, all in the same year!

Most importantly, Alan has helped bring the history of Gateshead right up to date, including mentions of some of our most notable events – like the Queen's opening of the Gateshead Millennium Bridge.

And unlike some local histories, which can get rather bogged down in dates and details, Alan has provided this volume with a sense of humour, and selected some of the more light-hearted moments. So when he quite rightly documents the building of the Angel of the North, an event which is already passing into our modern history, he does not overlook the fact that one of Gateshead's finest hours was our victory in *It's a Knockout* in the 1980s!

Because Gateshead has changed so much in the last decade, it is easy to forget that for newcomers to the area and the next generation of youngsters their Gateshead is a very different place from the one I grew up in.

It is an exhilarating time for us with so many new things now taking shape here on Gateshead Quays. But it is important that at a time of such rapid change we do not forget our past. While we look forward to the new, we should not forget the old – our heritage. Preserving and celebrating this rich, colourful history through books such as this ensures they still remain important parts of our future even when they have passed out of living memory.

Mick Henry
Leader, Gateshead Council

Introduction and Acknowledgements

One problem in writing about Gateshead is that the area covered by that name has changed substantially in recent years. Prior to 1974, the County Borough of Gateshead was a fairly compact, largely built-up area with a population of around 90,000, but in that year local government reorganisation resulted in this 'old' Gateshead being absorbed into a much larger Metropolitan Borough of Gateshead covering several times the area, much of it rural, and with a population of around 200,000. Other local councils which were absorbed into this 'greater Gateshead' included, in the main, those which had been associated with the former Gateshead Poor Law Union – Felling, Whickham, Blaydon and Ryton – together with Birtley to the south. My previous book of archive photographs concentrated on 'old' Gateshead, and while this book does the same, it also includes references to the other areas now incorporated in the 'new' Gateshead where this has seemed appropriate.

As with other towns close to larger neighbours – Birkenhead to Liverpool, Salford to Manchester – so Gateshead has always been overshadowed by its neighbour to the north, Newcastle upon Tyne. Indeed, over the centuries, Newcastle has made more than one attempt to annex Gateshead, one of which actually succeeded for a short time in the mid-sixteenth century. Although Gateshead managed to regain its political independence at that time, its economy continued to be dominated by Newcastle, and it is only within the last quarter of the twentieth century that it has really begun to emerge as a major player in its own right.

Gateshead today is quite different from the town which existed as recently as twenty-five years ago. This book attempts to describe the town's history from the days when it was written off as 'a dirty lane leading to Newcastle' to the modern Gateshead famous for its International Stadium, Angel of the North, Metro Centre, Millennium Bridge, Baltic Centre for Contemporary Art and the Sage Music Centre.

As with my previous books, I must express my thanks to the staff of Gateshead Central Library, notably Anthea Lang of the Local Studies

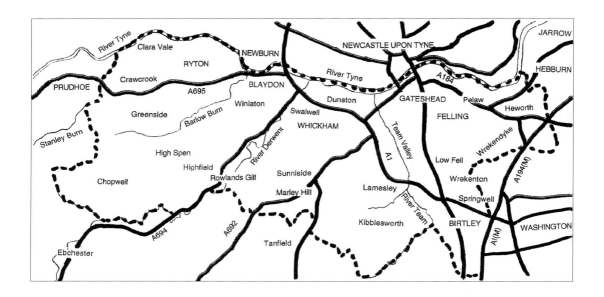

Outline map of the
Gateshead area.

Department and her predecessor Eileen Carnaffin, for their considerable assistance with information, and access to their large collection of photographs and maps. Some colour photographs were kindly supplied by Gateshead Council Press Office.

Alan Brazendale, 2004

chapter one

Pre-industrial Gateshead

Origins

The modern Metropolitan Borough of Gateshead probably began life as a number of small settlements along the south side of the River Tyne. Some were at the mouths of tributaries of the Tyne like Dunston (River Team) and Swalwell (River Derwent), where fishing provided additions to the diet, while others were located on defensible high ground like Winlaton and Whickham.

Almost nothing is known about the history of the area prior to Roman times, and until recently little more was known about the period following the arrival of the Romans, although it has always been accepted that a settlement of some sort must have existed at the southern end of the Roman bridge across the river. Although such a settlement must obviously have been overshadowed by the major fort at Newcastle, the discovery of a number of artefacts on the Gateshead side has suggested that this settlement may have been of much greater significance than was previously believed.

In some ways, Gateshead may also have served as an important 'communication centre' – a role it would also serve as a railway town many years in the future. The major Roman road from the south ran through Chester-le-Street and over Gateshead Fell to the river and although it was accepted for many years that Gateshead acquired its name as a corruption of 'Goats Head', meaning a headland roamed by, or sacred to, wild goats, an alternative suggestion is that it means the 'head of the road (gate)', i.e. where the road ended at the river.

At the point where Wrekenton now stands in the south of Gateshead, the Wrekendyke (another former Roman road) branches off the main north/south road and runs in a north-easterly direction towards Arbeia, the Roman supply base at what is now South Shields. Some sort of Roman presence at this road junction also seems likely.

The most striking evidence of Roman activity in the area, however, is undoubtedly the existence of Whickham Washingwell Fort which was

9

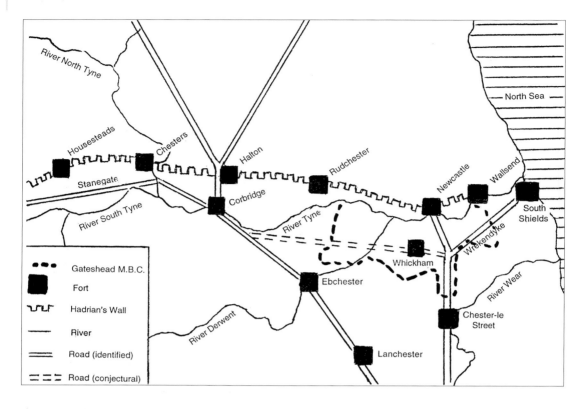

The Roman presence in Gateshead.

discovered by Professor Norman McCord. Professor McCord was flying over Whickham in 1970 en route to photograph some known Roman sites when he noticed the typical 'playing card' shape of a Roman fort in crop markings in fields near Washingwell Wood. His aerial photographs of the site led to some serious re-thinking of previous beliefs about the Roman frontier region.

Prior to this discovery, interest in the Roman presence on Tyneside had concentrated on the Roman forts in Newcastle and along Hadrian's Wall to the east and west – all north of the River Tyne. The route of the Stanegate – the Roman frontier before the construction of Hadrian's Wall – had never been traced to the east of Corbridge, but had always been sought on the north side of the Tyne. The discovery of the Washingwell fort suggested the possibility that the Stanegate had actually run to the south of the Tyne, with the Wrekendyke as its eastern end.

While it is to be hoped that future research will reveal further information about the Roman presence in Gateshead, it seems likely that coal mining and other industrial activity over the centuries will have destroyed much potential evidence.

The earliest recorded reference to Gateshead appeared long after the Roman Empire had crumbled, in Bede's seventh-century *History of the English Church and People* where he refers to 'Utta, a well-known priest and Abbot of Gateshead'. Clearly, there was a monastery in the area at that time, but whether there was any significant settlement around the monastery is not known.

Norman Gateshead

There was certainly an established local community in Gateshead by 1080 because in that year Walcher, the first Norman Bishop of Durham, was killed outside the local church. The murder appears to have been by way of reprisal following the murder of Liulph, a Saxon nobleman and ancestor of the Lumleys of Lumley Castle, who had been protesting against the oppressive tax collection methods of the Bishop's agents. When Walcher visited Gateshead in a gesture of appeasement, a crowd of local people demonstrated their hostility and the Bishop and his followers took refuge in the church, but the crowd set the building on fire and subsequently killed the Normans as they fled from the burning building.

This incident provoked a general uprising which was short-lived, as the Conqueror sent an army which laid waste to the whole area.

Despite this unfortunate start, Gateshead seems to have flourished under the Normans and had grown into a substantial community by the end of the twelfth century. Gateshead itself, which was owned by the Bishop, and the neighbouring Heworth, which belonged to the Prior and convent of Durham, were largely forest and provided good hunting facilities. In consequence, the area became a favoured resort of successive Bishops.

The town's first charter, in 1164, defined the respective rights and duties of the Bishop's forester and the town's burgesses, and suggests that the town was at least some way towards becoming a borough in its own right. It confirmed the right of burgesses to take bracken, brushwood and the like from the forest for their own use in return for appropriate payment, and the right of pasture etc. on the common lands of Saltwell, but stopped short of establishing a chief official or a borough court.

A few years later, in 1183, the then Bishop ordered his own 'Domesday Book' survey of the Bishopric, known as the Boldon Book, which gave the following information about the town:

> Gateshead, with borough, mills, fisheries and bakehouses, and with three parts of the arable land renders 60 marks. The fourth part of the arable land, with the assarts [clearings in the forest] which the Bishop caused to be made, and the meadows, are in the hands of the lord Bishop with the stock of two ploughs. Osmund's land renders 22 shillings and six pence.

This brief reference nevertheless indicates Gateshead's growing importance. It appears to have been the milling centre for North Durham at the time, and the mills may have included early windmills on Windmill Hills as well as watermills on the Tyne and its tributaries. Apart from Gateshead, only Durham and Darlington appear to have had communal bakehouses controlled by the Bishop. The fishing was also an important element in the local economy and was to be the subject of future disputes with Newcastle.

By this time Durham was recognised as a County Palatine, almost a state within a state – with the Bishop as a virtual local sovereign. Gateshead, like the

rest of the county, was predominantly an agricultural area and its history around this time is essentially one of slow but steady growth despite regular harassment from the north side of the river, ranging from interference with fishing rights to attempts to take control of the growing town and its markets. In the fourteenth century, however, this friction became more significant with the development of the coal-mining industry.

The long history of farming in Gateshead. Threshing with a steam engine, c. 1920.

Relations with Newcastle

As Gateshead prospered, relations between Gateshead and Newcastle became difficult as Newcastle saw the town on the other side of the river as a threat, and this hostility was to have a considerable impact on the development of the borough.

Under the Normans, the Tyne had been officially recognised as the boundary between Durham and Northumberland, with the southern third of the river being regarded as belonging to Durham, the northern third as Northumberland's and the middle third as common property. This had particular relevance where Gateshead and Newcastle faced each other at either end of the sole bridge over the Tyne. As Newcastle grew in strength, however, it increasingly attempted to exert control over the whole river and settlements on both sides of it down to the sea.

In the case of Gateshead, this interference was initially directed at control of the bridge and the fisheries in Gateshead, but was later extended to attempting to restrict activities like public markets and shipbuilding. Inquiries in 1293 and 1317 confirmed the original boundary, but a further inquiry proved necessary in 1322 when Newcastle merchants destroyed some of the Bishop's fisheries on

Gateshead from Newcastle in 1835.

the Tyne, another in 1336 after Pipewellgate fishermen had been forced to sell their catch in Newcastle and yet another in 1345 after Newcastle burgesses had seized five ships carrying goods between Whickham and Gateshead. All these inquiries found in Gateshead's favour, as did royal decisions regarding free shipment on the river in 1383 and 1393, but eventually the tide (perhaps a particularly appropriate word here) began to turn in Newcastle's favour.

In 1383, Newcastle built a fortified tower at the south (i.e. Gateshead) end of the bridge which was not removed until 1416 despite protests by the Bishop, and in 1454 King Henry VI reversed decisions of his predecessor and granted control of the Tyne to Newcastle. At the time this seemed to satisfy Newcastle's objectives. A hundred years later, however, the profitability of the coal-mining areas of Gateshead and Whickham raised the stakes significantly, and Newcastle sought the complete annexation of Gateshead.

chapter two

The coal-mining era

The development of coal-mining

Coal mining was the first great industry to develop in Gateshead and dominated the local economy from the fifteenth century, reaching a peak in the seventeenth century and then continuing, albeit at a much reduced level, into the twentieth century. The last collieries to close within the boundaries of the old borough were Sheriff Hill and Redheugh which closed in 1926 and 1927 respectively, but collieries in the outlying areas lingered even longer; Marley Hill Colliery, south of Whickham, closed as late as 1983. During the earlier period, the twin manors of Gateshead and Whickham, the latter now part of modern Gateshead, were linked together in what was known, for coal-mining purposes, as the Grand Lease, and produced more coal per annum than any area of equal size anywhere in the world.

Coal had been used as a domestic fuel since Roman times, generally collected from the banks of rivers wherever it outcropped, but it had no particular advantage over wood which was freely available. In consequence, the use of coal remained a very small-scale activity. This situation began to change in the fourteenth century as the demand for fuel for early industrial activities began to grow and supplies of wood dwindled and became more expensive, a process which accelerated in later centuries as the Industrial Revolution gathered pace.

Among mining areas, Tyneside had a number of initial advantages. Not only were the first seams to be exploited near the surface and therefore easier to access, but they were close to the Tyne which offered a cheap and efficient means of transport before the development of modern roads and railways. Coal was carried from the pits to staiths on the riverside, where it was loaded into shallow boats known as keels. These transported it down to the deeper water near the mouth of the river for transhipment into ocean-going vessels. In consequence, during the fourteenth and fifteenth centuries the combined manors of Gateshead and Whickham became one of the few areas where coal was transported more than a few miles from its source and earned more than a few pounds per annum in sales.

Mineral rights in the area were initially held by the Bishop of Durham and the earliest known lease for coal-mining purposes took place in 1344 when the Bishop leased coal mines within the two manors to Sir Thomas Grey and the Rector of Whickham. Other leases followed which included wayleaves allowing coal to be transported over farmland to the Tyne.

As already indicated, coal was originally collected where it outcropped on the banks of the river, and in due course this led to drifts or tunnels being driven into the bankside to get access to the shallow seams. As the coal seams dipped away from the bankside, it became more appropriate to sink vertical shafts down to the coal. Initially these were of the 'bell-pit' type, where shallow shafts were dug down to the level at which coal occurred and then worked sideways as far as was safe. Another shaft would then be sunk a short distance away and the process repeated. In practice, of course, the unproductive time and labour involved in sinking each shaft to a depth of perhaps 30 feet meant that there was always a temptation to keep extracting coal rather further away from the shaft than was really safe. There are many references in church and other records of the time to men being 'slayne in a pit' of this type.

Output from drifts and 'bell-pits' was necessarily small and the industry remained small-scale throughout the fifteenth century. By the end of the century, however, the demand for coal for new and expanding industries was such that it became necessary to get access to seams which were deeper and, because of the way the coal seams tilted, further away from the river. This change led to the development of a great deal of new technology, much of which gradually 'spilled over' into other industries.

The capital cost of sinking deep shafts meant that, in order to get an adequate return on the initial investment, it became necessary to extract coal at considerable distances from the shaft. This change led, for example, to the

left A faceworker at Wardley Colliery in 1900.

right Chopwell Colliery in 1908. A famous name in coal-mining history.

development of roof support systems, the use of small wheeled vehicles (known as 'tubs') to move coal from the working face to the bottom of the shaft, winding gear to move men, coal and materials up and down the shaft, and ventilation systems to circulate air round the workings.

The deep pits also experienced problems with flooding, particularly in collieries near the river, and the development of pumps capable of dealing with the problem represented a major breakthrough in extending the lives of many pits. From around 1820 onwards, for example, the Tyne Main Colliery at Friar's

top Addison Colliery in 1931. The Addison Male Voice Choir continues to bear its name.

above Felling John Pit. The site of the 1812 disaster.

Goose was served by a 180hp pumping engine capable of drawing off nearly 1½ million gallons of water per day. The ruins of the building which housed the Friar's Goose pumping engine still stand today.

Felling Colliery is a grim illustration of this stage in the history of the mining industry. A new 'downcast' shaft had been sunk in 1810/11 to get access to deeper seams which had become more accessible through the development of more powerful steam engines to operate pumps and winding engines. Ventilation, however, was still provided by a fire at the nearby 'upcast' shaft to draw air through the workings. In 1812, there was a tremendous explosion which resulted in the deaths of ninety-one men and boys, and a further explosion in 1813 killed another twenty-two men.

These disasters contributed to an increased interest in mining safety and led to the development of safety lamps by both George Stephenson and Humphrey Davy, a prototype of the Davy lamp being tested in the nearby Hebburn Colliery.

Another important development, however, took place on the surface – the development of the wooden wagonway.

Wooden wagonways

As coal-mining moved away from the river, a major transport problem arose in how to get the coal from the pit to the river. In the early days pack-horses were used, but these carried relatively small quantities of coal which led to their being superseded in due course by wains – wagons drawn by horses or oxen and capable of carrying up to a ton of coal at a time. In days long before modern roads existed, both these methods entailed crossing fields which were turned into quagmires in winter and dust-bowls in summer, making movement across them increasingly difficult and doing considerable damage to the crops through which they passed. In the late seventeenth and early eighteenth centuries, for example, at least 700 wains were in use in the Whickham area alone and the damage done to agricultural land can be imagined. Landowners were also in a position to demand ever-higher wayleave rents for the right to pass over their lands. All these factors created a demand for a cheaper and more efficient transport system. The answer was the wooden wagonway.

A loaded wagon on a downhill run in 1773. Staiths are visible on the left-hand side.

In many ways, wooden wagonways were like their later offspring the railways but they differed in a number of important respects. Like railways they involved vehicles running along rails, but the rails and the wheels of the vehicles were of wood rather than iron, and traction was provided by men or horses rather than steam. Later experience led to tracks being designed to make the maximum use of gravity, and wagonways which survived long enough were converted to use steam power, often in the form of stationery steam engines, and devices like the self-acting incline where the weight of descending loaded wagons was used to pull up empty wagons.

Although Tyneside mine owners were probably not the originators of this system of transport, they were certainly amongst the first to use it. The

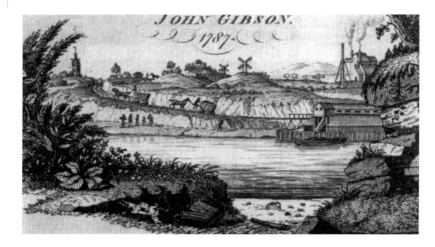

Windmill Hills in 1787. A
certain amount of artistic
licence is evident.

A rope-operated incline in
Birtley around the end of the
nineteenth century.

A fully operational railway
system at Greenside Colliery
in 1931.

Whickham Grand Lease wagonway, carrying coals from the eastern areas of Whickham down to the river at Dunston, appears to have been in existence by the 1620s and the Stella Grand Lease way linking Ryton collieries to the river at Stella by the 1630s. Other wagonways which were constructed by the end of the seventeenth century included the Chopwell, Clavering, Cowclose, Crawcrook and Winlaton ways in the Ryton area and the Dunston, Ravensworth, Riding Field and Teams ways in Whickham. In the Gateshead and Felling areas the Bensham, Felling and Parkmoor, Sheriff Hill and Gateshead Fell wagonways also came into existence around this time.

In the early eighteenth century, the exploitation of coal resources further south led to development of new ways either side of the Derwent running down to new staiths at Derwenthaugh – the Bucksnook, Old Western and New Western Ways. In 1725 the most famous wagonway of all, the Tanfield, came into existence, part of its route lying over that of another early wagonway and feeding staiths at Dunston and Redheugh. This was progressively modernised over the years to include the Causey Arch, the oldest stone railway bridge in the world dating from 1727, self-acting inclines, stationery steam engines, and eventually locomotives, finally closing as recently as 1964. Part of it has since been re-opened and is now operated by a steam preservation society.

The Tanfield was unique for its long working life, which has left ample evidence of its existence. Other wagonways had very short lives, sometimes as little as twenty years or less, and the evidence of their existence is fairly sparse although there are exceptions, notably in Whickham. Two stretches of wagonway which survived until the second half of the twentieth century, albeit much modified, were the Bowes Railway, which incorporated a number of stretches of old wagonway and part of which is also preserved, and a short length of the route of the New Western Way which was still in use serving the Derwenthaugh Cokeworks until their recent closure.

left Old staiths at Bill Quay.

right The more modern Dunston staiths in 1977 (still standing today).

Annexation by Newcastle

In the sixteenth century, the profitability of the mines in Gateshead, at that time the most productive coalfield in the world, made them pawns in high-level politics and reinvigorated the centuries-old friction between Gateshead and Newcastle.

In the early 1550s, John Dudley, Duke of Northumberland and Lord Protector under Edward VI, was in the process of creating a power base in the North of England. The Bishop of Durham had been imprisoned, which left Gateshead undefended. In March 1553, two Acts were rushed through Parliament to replace the see of Durham with two new sees of Durham and Newcastle and to annex Gateshead to Newcastle. The preamble to the Annexation Act is interesting because of its abuse of the inhabitants of Gateshead who were alleged to commit 'manifold enormities and disorders' in Newcastle before escaping back to Gateshead, besides dumping rubbish in the Tyne and failing to repair their end of the bridge.

The Acts did not remain in force for long. Edward VI died later in 1553 and was succeeded by Mary; Dudley was beheaded following his attempt to place Lady Jane Grey on the throne, and the Bishop was released from the Tower and reinstated. The two Acts were repealed in April 1554, but only after opponents, led by Newcastle merchants, had been bought off by ceding control of both the valuable Saltmeadows riverside area of Gateshead and the Gateshead tolls for insignificant sums.

In 1574 and 1576, Newcastle made further attempts to annex Gateshead but were successfully resisted by the people of Gateshead using a variety of means, including a petition to Lord Burghley and an address to the Speaker of the House of Commons.

Unfortunately, although Gateshead appeared to have defeated Newcastle, this proved to be something of a pyrrhic victory because of the manipulations between 1577 and 1582 of Thomas Sutton, Master of the Ordnance at Berwick. Through the patronage of the Earl of Leicester, Queen Elizabeth's favourite, Sutton was able to transfer the lease of the Grand Lease coal mines of Gateshead and Whickham from the Bishop to the Queen for a nominal rent (which Sutton paid) and then from the Queen to a small group of Newcastle merchants. Although the loss of income to the Bishop was enormous, the more intensive exploitation by Newcastle over the next century meant that coal shipments increased more than ten times from under 60,000 tons to over 600,000 tons a year, which led to increases in the population of Gateshead which more than doubled over the same period.

When the lease expired in 1679, however, the seams of good-quality coal were almost exhausted, and Gateshead was very much a town in decline.

Religious struggles

Annexation was not the only political issue affecting Gateshead and coal-mining around this time. In the sixteenth and seventeenth centuries, events in the North East reflected the religious struggles which were convulsing the nation.

In 1569, the Earls of Northumberland and Westmorland led a rebellion intended to re-establish the Roman Catholic religion and release Mary, Queen of Scots, from her imprisonment. The rebellion was initially successful, but when faced with much larger forces led by the Earls of Essex and Warwick, and with another army led by George Bowes (an ancestor of the mine-owning Bowes family of Gibside) in their rear, they accepted that defeat was inevitable and retreated to the relative safety of the dales north of the border. The Government's retribution was carried out with great severity. George Bowes subsequently boasted that there was hardly a town or village in Durham (which included Gateshead and its surrounding communities) in which he had not executed at least one of the inhabitants.

In 1640, the English were defeated by a Scots Presbyterian army at the Battle of Newburn (or Stella Haughs) between Blaydon and Ryton. After this defeat, the English camped behind the church in Whickham but set fire to their tents when the Scots pursued them up the hill and inadvertently set fire to an outcrop of coal which subsequently continued to burn for many years. The Scots then pressed on to Newcastle, which decided that it did not have the resources to defend itself against superior odds. In consequence, the town's garrison retreated to Durham, taking with it those guns and ammunition it was able to carry and dumping the rest in the river.

The subsequent occupation of Newcastle by the Scots was fairly peaceful in the town itself but had a disastrous effect on the coal trade, which was brought to a halt, and on shops, many of which were closed. On the Gateshead side of the river, the Scots attacked the mines belonging to Sir Thomas Liddell and 'seized his coals, broke his colliery engines, drowned and destroyed the best part of his coal', damage which took some time to repair when the Scots finally withdrew after being bought off by Parliament for £300,000.

The long-standing hostility between King and Parliament finally broke out into civil war in 1642, and in the following year an agreement was reached between Parliamentary and Scots forces (the 'Solemn League and Covenant'). This led, in early 1644, to a siege of Newcastle by a Scots army which lasted for several months. Once again, coal 'exports' to London (a Parliamentary strong-hold) were stopped. The coal industry was, however, involved indirectly in the siege because the Scots constructed a temporary bridge of keels to bypass the only bridge across the river.

The Parliamentary victory at the Battle of Marston Moor, in which Parliamentary and Scots forces fought together for the first time, freed around 10,000 Scots soldiers to return to the attack on Newcastle. In July 1644, there was a battle on the Windmill Hills in Gateshead between the Scots and Newcastle forces. After an unsuccessful preliminary assault by an advance group of Scots, Cromwell himself took command and threw the Royalist forces off the hill, chasing them down into Gateshead itself and back across the bridge. He then laid renewed siege to Newcastle, mounting five batteries of cannon on Windmill Hills from which he bombarded the town, which finally surrendered in October 1644. St Mary's Church Vestry Minute Book records the

damage done in Gateshead by the Scots army, including removing cattle from Gateshead Fell (where they had been sent for safekeeping away from the fighting), destroying the rectory and damaging the church itself.

Cromwell visited Gateshead again in 1650 when he rested overnight in Whickham en route to his defeat of the Scots at the Battle of Dunbar.

Dockendale Hall in Whickham where Cromwell is believed to have stayed en route to the Battle of Dunbar.

chapter three

Other industries

Changing industry

Although coal-mining had dominated Gateshead's economy for many years and its decline clearly had adverse consequences for the town, other industries had existed in the borough, sometimes for centuries, and these continued, and in some cases expanded, as coal-mining declined. The town also saw the intro-duction of new trades, some of which were accurately described as 'noxious' trades, possibly provoking the well-known description of Gateshead as 'a dirty lane leading to Newcastle'. Although these changes brought a revival in the town's economic fortunes during the nineteenth century, this proved to be only temporary, with many of the new industries declining towards the end of the century and in the early twentieth century.

It is not possible to include a comprehensive account of these changes in a short general history but the following paragraphs are intended to indicate the main trends.

Traditional industries

Among the traditional industries in the town, milling had been carried on since medieval times. As early as the time of the Boldon Book in 1183, Gateshead was one of the milling centres for Durham and continued to flourish as such, with both windmills and watermills, right up to the end of the eighteenth century. As the name suggests, Windmill Hills was the site of several mills (still probably as many as ten in the early nineteenth century) and there were others at Carr Hill. By the end of the nineteenth century, however, no working mills remained and most of the buildings had already been demolished.

Quarrying for grindstones had also been carried on since the Middle Ages, mainly on Gateshead Fell and in the Eighton Banks area, but by the eighteenth century suitable stone was almost worked out and the trade shifted elsewhere.

Quarrying for building stone continued into the nineteenth century but by the end of that century most quarries had been closed, filled in and built over.

The pottery industry was also well established in the Middle Ages but thereafter seems to have disappeared for some reason until a revival in the middle of the eighteenth century, when a number of new potteries were introduced. Most of these were fairly small, the two largest being at Carr Hill, which closed in 1893, and at Sheriff Hill (near the Old Cannon Inn) which closed in 1909. A Government-sponsored pottery project in the 1950s was unsuccessful.

Boat-building, mainly small-scale, also had a long history in Gateshead despite strong opposition from Newcastle which wished to exercise monopoly rights in this area. Until the seventeenth century, work was limited to the building of small craft like keels, and associated activities such as block- and mast-making, rope-making (see below) and ship's chandlers, but in the 1750s some firms began building sea-going craft. The industry survived into the twentieth century without ever becoming a major factor in the town's economy. One interesting event occurred in 1821, however, when James Smith, a chain-maker at Hawks' Ironworks, built an iron rowing-boat named *Vulcan* which was claimed to be the first ever iron boat. The occasion appears to have raised little interest at the time and James Smith was drowned shortly afterwards in an accident where it was suggested that the crew had 'too much beer and too little ballast'. The boat appears to have been left to rust away.

Both shipbuilding and coal-mining need rope but when rope-making began in Gateshead (as against Newcastle) is uncertain. There was certainly a rope-walk in Hillgate as early as the late seventeenth century but this belonged to a

above The Pipewellgate area of mixed industry, shops and housing.

opposite
above left A last survivor of milling – the mill in Whickham Chase Park.

above right A ship repair yard at Bill Quay, c. 1920.

below Quarrying in Windy Nook in the early twentieth century.

Newcastle rope-maker. Thereafter, several rope-making firms were established in the eighteenth and nineteenth centuries. The best-known Gateshead firm of rope-makers was probably Haggie Brothers, which was established in 1800 and in 1845 was able to produce a 3-mile long rope weighing 13 tons for the Liverpool & Manchester Railway. The members of the firm were prominent public figures, one of them, David Haggie, becoming Mayor in 1853. The firm became part of British Ropes in 1926. Haggie's main competitors were R.S. Newall & Company and Dixon Corbitt which amalgamated in 1887 and also became part of British Ropes in 1959.

Clay pipe-making was an industry for which Gateshead was at one time a major centre. The industry was certainly in existence in 1646, when parish records show the burial of a pipe-maker named William Sewell, and continued until George Stonehouse, the last of the Gateshead pipe-makers, closed his shop in 1935. Establishing the number of pipe-makers at any one time between those dates is difficult because it was a business in which 'amateurs' flourished, but in 1675 they were important enough to form part of a guild, and in 1838 there were ten pipe-makers. Probably the most prominent pipe-maker from an historical point of view was Frank J. Finn, who became Mayor in 1898.

Iron manufacture and engineering

Iron manufacturing, engineering and chemicals were the new industries which dominated the Gateshead economy in the nineteenth century.

Iron manufacturing in the Gateshead area dates back to around 1682, when Sir Ambrose Crowley established iron works in Winlaton which were later extended to Swalwell, Blaydon and the Teams. Crowley's manufactured a huge number of iron products, ranging from nails to armaments, and was initially very successful, but the failure to specialise is probably the key factor which led to the eventual failure of the company when faced with competition from smaller, more specialised firms in later years. Apart from his initial business success, however, Crowley is best known for the range of forward-looking policies he used to manage his business, which were many years ahead of his time. He introduced a 'code of laws' for his employees, a pension scheme, 'Crowley's Court' which was a sort of early industrial tribunal, personnel records, a company doctor and a chaplain. His employees tended to be strong Tories in the early years and acted as a group known as 'Crowley's Crew', always ready to take on more radical groups such as the keelmen.

William Hawks, a former employee of Crowley's, set up in competition in 1747 and followed some of Crowley's paternalistic policies. Probably the firm's longest-lasting memorial is the High Level Bridge over the Tyne which was built between 1846 and 1849 under the guidance of George and Robert Stephenson. Like Crowley's employees, Hawks' employees, who were Whigs, tended to band together outside work as 'Haaks's Men', from time to time in conflict with Crowley's Crew, and who were claimed to have 'won the Battle of Watterloo'. Competition between the Crowley and Hawks businesses was another factor leading to the gradual decline of Crowley's, but Hawks themselves suffered from the same failure to specialise (they built bridges in other parts of the world along with steam engines, dredgers and lighthouses) and finally closed in 1889.

A third large iron manufacturer, although not in the same league as Crowley's and Hawks, was John Abbot & Company, which started in business in 1835 and closed down in 1909, probably because of the same lack of specialisation.

One large firm which did not suffer the same fate was Clarke Chapman, which was set up at the South Shore in the early 1860s and continues to the present day. The reasons for the company's continuing success may well be a record of successful innovation and an avoidance of an excessive range of activities. In 1877, Charles Parsons joined the company and conducted his initial experiments with the steam turbine at the works, and the firm later collaborated with Joseph Swan in the manufacture of carbon filament electric light bulbs.

While three of these large firms were driven out of business by competition from smaller, more efficient competitors, a reverse trend occurred in the field of locomotive engineering where one large firm emerged at the end of the nineteenth century as the dominant player in the field. This was the Greenesfield Locomotive Works established by the North Eastern Railway Company in 1852. Initially, Greenesfield's function was to repair existing locomotives, but this was later expanded to include the large-scale manufacture of new locomotives. The numbers employed grew rapidly and by the end of the century Greenesfield was by far the largest employer in Gateshead. Unfortunately it became a victim of its own success. In 1909, it became apparent that further expansion was impossible on the cramped site and locomotive building was transferred to Darlington, reducing the number employed at Greenesfield from 3,300 to 1,500. In 1932, when over 1,000 were still employed there on locomotive repair work, the LNER decided to close the works completely, although they were brought back into use for a time during the Second World War and immediate post-war period.

Chemicals

A number of chemical factories were set up at the South Shore and Friar's Goose areas of Gateshead in the 1820s and 1830s which manufactured a range of products including soap, glue, dyes, soda, bicarbonate of soda and Epsom salts.

Coopers making wooden casks for zinc oxide at Birtley, early 1920s.

Charles Allhusen acquired and amalgamated the various works in the South Shore area in 1840 to form a large manufacturing unit always known as 'Allhusen's' despite subsequent changes of ownership. In 1891, both the South Shore and Friar's Goose sites were acquired by the United Alkali Company, which closed down the Friar's Goose site before the First World War and gradually ran down operations at the South Shore area in favour of Teesside. United Alkali became part of ICI in 1926.

Glass-making was a natural development in the area, using local coal supplies and sand brought back as ballast in colliers returning from the Thames, and records indicate that glass-making in Gateshead dates back as far as the mid-eighteenth century. The industry was in decline by the mid-nineteenth century and by the end of the nineteenth century only two main firms remained – Sowerby's and George Davidson – both manufacturing pressed-glass products which imitated cut glass.

Depression

To summarise the situation around the late nineteenth and early twentieth centuries, some of the major employers in Gateshead had either closed altogether, like most of the big engineering firms, or moved the bulk of their operations elsewhere, like the North Eastern Railway Company. The effect of these losses was obscured by the artificial boost to the economy provided by the First World War, but during the 1920s the depression deepened as the chemical industry moved away to Teesside and the last of the collieries closed. The North Eastern Railway Works closed completely in 1932.

opposite South Shore, centre of the chemical industry in 1880.

right A firm which survived. CWS packing room at Pelaw in 1930.

In 1934, a Government investigation into the 'derelict areas' found that the damage caused by industrial decline had many aspects. In addition to the obvious poverty of individuals and families resulting from the lack of work, there were often serious psychological consequences, with individuals losing confidence in their own abilities. The absence of the necessary finance also meant that the local authorities lacked the resources to spend on attracting new industries which were, in any case, disinclined to invest in areas labelled as 'derelict' or 'distressed'. Intervention at national level was clearly necessary.

One of the solutions proposed was the creation of trading estates providing ready-made factories with power supplies already laid on. By 1935, it had been decided that the first such trading estate should be established in the North East. There was initially some in-fighting between the interested local authorities to accommodate the proposed estate and, once Gateshead had been decided upon, there was more disagreement over whether the estate should be built in Team Valley or Saltmeadows. In 1936, Team Valley was selected as the preferred site and a development company was set up.

Team Valley Trading Estate

The Team Valley site consisted of 700 acres of low-lying pasture and was subject to flooding in wet weather. It was stabilised with millions of tons of colliery waste, a device which managed to deal with two problems at the same time, albeit at considerable cost. The site adjoined the main north/south railway line, and road access was quickly developed which has since been improved with links to the A1 (Western Bypass). The River Team was canalised and cleaned, and the estate roads were laid out in a grid pattern, the main north/south road (Kingsway) being constructed as a dual carriageway 174 feet wide, making it the widest road in the country at that time. Parallel roads were also constructed called, as might be expected, Queensway, Princesway, Dukesway and Earlsway. Starting at the north end the crossing east/west roads were named First Avenue, Second Avenue and so on, which at least made it easy for delivery vehicles to find their way round such a large estate. In addition to the access points at the north and south ends, another road (Eastern Avenue) was built to link the centre with Low Fell.

The first factory was rented out in September 1936 and by the time of the Second World War, 15,000 people were employed on the estate. In the period since then, the estate has continued to develop although mainly in the fields of light engineering, shopping and offices rather than heavy industry, and it continues to play a significant role in employment in the Gateshead area.

In the Saltmeadows area, a much smaller trading area has been developed since the end of the Second World War, and further developments are now taking place in the Gateshead Quays area as described in chapter 9.

chapter four

Years of growth and change

The population explosion

Although it is difficult to visualise these days, prior to the nineteenth century most of the area of modern Gateshead was thinly populated with those engaged in farming, coal-mining or other localised activities like quarrying, located in small villages spread throughout the countryside. The bulk of the population was concentrated in the riverside area centred on Bottle Bank, with Bridge Street, Bankwell Stairs, Mirk Lane and other passageways running up and down the bank and Pipewellgate and Hillgate running east and west alongside the river. The houses in this area were huddled together cheek by jowl with industrial concerns, some of them carrying on the 'noxious trades' referred to in the previous chapter, and tended to be in very poor condition – damp and dirty and lacking the most basic amenities. A medical report of 1850 reported that: 'The subsoil on the sloping side of the hill is damp and most foul, the brickwork of the buildings is ruinous, the timber rotten, and an appearance of general decay pervades the whole district.'

Severe overcrowding added to these problems. In one particularly bad case, a single house in Hillgate in the mid-nineteenth century contained sixteen families totalling seventy-one people. Conditions elsewhere were almost as bad. Sanitation was almost non-existent, consisting of middens, which were drained, if at all, by open sewers. In these circumstances, it is not surprising that the first cholera epidemic in 1831/32 (there were others in 1849 and 1853) caused 234 deaths, and typhus was a recurring problem. It was the first epidemic that led, in 1832, to the building of the Gateshead Dispensary, which was financed by public subscription and provided medical care to the sick poor prior to the introduction of the National Health Service.

For most of the sixteenth century, the population of this 'old' Gateshead was fairly constant at under 2,000, and although this increased with the great expansion of coal-mining it had still only reached 6,000 by the end of the seventeenth century and was still under 7,000 at the end of the eighteenth

century. Around the beginning of the nineteenth century, however, the continued growth of industry and population created an increased demand for better-quality housing, and people who could afford it began to move away from the riverside area, so that by the middle of the century the northern ends of what are now High Street and West Street were largely built up. This growth was limited, however, by the continued existence of great landed estates and the town fields of Windmill Hills and Bensham controlled by the borough-holders (property-owners) and freemen (members of trade guilds). These hemmed in the growing town, particularly on the west, while to the south lay the largely uncultivated area of Gateshead Fell over which the borough-holders and freemen held pasturage rights.

As the nineteenth century progressed, these problems were resolved, partly by a process of enclosure and partly by the gradual decline of the great estates.

Enclosures

The town fields and more limited rights on Gateshead Fell had at one time belonged to all the citizens of Gateshead but had come under the control of the borough-holders and freemen at some time in the past, initially as representatives of the community. Between 1807 and 1814 these 'representatives' sought and obtained Acts of Parliament to enclose the Fell and the town fields in Bensham so that they could divide the land up amongst themselves (a common practice at the time). This process proved to be quite complicated (there were, for example, 200 claims for land on Gateshead Fell alone) and the process was not completed until 1822. This effectively cleared the land for building development.

Gateshead Fell

The impact of enclosures was particularly dramatic on Gateshead Fell.

Around the end of the eighteenth century, Robert Surtees, the Durham historian, described the Fell as 'a wide, spongy, dark moor' which was covered with gorse and brambles, and the remains of early mineshafts, pit-heaps and quarries. It was inhabited by all kinds of vagrants who made a scanty living as tinkers, rag and bone men and the like, and lived in miserable dwellings made of earth and roofed with turf. That part of the road to Durham which passed over the Fell was in consequence known as Sodhouse Bank. Its wild nature, especially in winter, is described by John Wesley in a diary entry dated 23 February 1745:

> We found the roads abundantly worse than they had been the day before; not only because the snows were deeper, which made the causeways in many places unpassable, but likewise because the hard frost, succeeding the thaw, had made all the ground like glass. We were often obliged to walk, it being impossible to ride, and our horses several times fell down while we were leading them, but not once

while we were riding them, during the whole journey. It was past 8 before we got to Gateshead Fell, which appeared a great pathless waste of white. The snow filling up and covering all the roads, we were at a loss how to proceed; when an honest man of Newcastle overtook and guided us safe into the town.

Many a rough journey I have had before, but one like this I never had; between wind, and hail, and ice, and snow, and driving sleet, and piercing cold.

To some extent the enclosures of the early nineteenth century merely formalised and legalised a process which had been going on for some time. In the middle of the seventeenth century, a survey determined the total acreage of the Fell to be 1,300 acres, but by the time of the enclosures this had shrunk by more than half.

The Commissioners who had been appointed to carry out the enclosures proceeded to make major improvements, removing pit-heaps, installing drains and laying out seven new roads and a site for a new church. On the negative side, ninety dwellings were demolished against considerable opposition from the occupants.

The results of this policy were quickly apparent. The population increased rapidly, with St John's Church the centre of a new Gateshead Fell parish. Low Fell became a fashionable place to live, with an active social life based on the Cannon Inn. High Fell grew in a rather different way, with the bulk of the population being pitmen and quarrymen, and the Three Tuns becoming a centre of radical politics. Other smaller villages and hamlets also developed at Blue Quarries, Carr Hill, Deckham, Sheriff Hill and Wrekenton. Eventually, however, all these settlements gradually merged into the Gateshead conurbation.

above The new, flatter,
Durham Road through Low
Fell, *c.* 1910.

right Grandfathers' Cottages
at Blue Quarries in 1938.

right below House on old
Sheriff Hill.

Park House, c. 1889.

The end of the great landed estates

The great estates which occupied most of the area of 'old' Gateshead until the nineteenth century were largely created during the thirteenth and fourteenth centuries and many of their names are still preserved in the districts, and sometimes the roads, of modern Gateshead. After their initial creation, they underwent many changes of both boundaries and owners over the centuries, but they continued to be occupied by members of the landed gentry until the late eighteenth and early nineteenth centuries when the rapidly encroaching evidence of the Industrial Revolution led to their being sold off to representatives of the new industrial aristocracy. By the end of the century, however, most of the industrialists had also moved on for similar reasons, leaving yet more land for building.

The Bishop of Durham's hunting park, which later became the Park estate, was a very large estate which originally occupied the whole of the town's eastern area from the High Street to the Felling boundary where it adjoined the hunting park of Heworth, belonging to the Prior and convent of Durham. Over the centuries, several smaller estates were split off including the Claxton, Friar's Goose and Saltmeadows estates, and the remainder of the estate became borough demesne land farmed by the lord of the manor. When William Cotesworth (after whom Coatsworth Road is named but misspelled) became lord of the manor in the eighteenth century, he made substantial improvements to the land and rebuilt Park House, the manor house.

In the nineteenth century, Park House was occupied by a series of industrialists until it was acquired by Clarke Chapman, the engineering firm, who turned it into offices. The remainder of the estate was developed partly for industrial purposes, notably by Clarke Chapman, and partly for housing. Interestingly, there was a local legend that Park House had served as a model for 'Gateshead Hall' in Charlotte Brontë's *Jane Eyre*, and although there seems to be no basis for this belief it did lead to a number of local streets being given names like Brontë Street and Jane Eyre Terrace.

left The 'Salte Welle' which gave its name to the Saltwellside estate.

right Saltwell Towers, built in 1876.

Another large estate was the Shipcote (meaning 'sheepfold') estate which consisted of the lands belonging to the Hospital of St Edmund, which later became Holy Trinity Church. These ran either side of Durham Road from approximately the present site of the Civic Centre to the vicinity of Kells Lane. This estate seems to have followed a reverse path to that of the Park estate, because when William Cotesworth acquired it in the early eighteenth century he discovered that substantial areas of common land had been absorbed into the estate in the seventeenth century. Later, in the eighteenth and nineteenth centuries, other small estates, including Whinney House and Field House, were also added. The land was progressively sold off, mainly for housing, although two farmhouses – Shipcote Farm, occupied by the Dryden family after whom Dryden Road is named, and Shipcote House – survived into the twentieth century and other parts became sites for the Leisure Centre, Central Library, Art Gallery and Fire Station.

Probably the largest estate, the name of which has particular significance in the history of Gateshead, was the Saltwellside estate which derived its name from the Salte Welle which still stands in Saltwell Park and comprised all the land sloping down from the Saltwell Park area to the River Team, from Bensham in the north to Low Fell in the south. The estate was split into smaller units in the nineteenth century which were known as Saltwell Hall, Saltwell Cottage and High Teams.

William Wailes, a glass manufacturer, built Saltwell Towers on the Saltwell Cottage estate which was subsequently acquired by the Council to form the basis for Saltwell Park. Many other local businessmen built large mansions on parts of the estate including R.S. Newall, the rope manufacturer, who built 'Ferndene' in the 1850s and had a private observatory in the grounds which contained what was, at the time, the largest telescope in the world. The High Teams estate was bought by the Gateshead Poor Law Union as a site for a new workhouse, part of the Saltwell Hall estate became Saltwell cemetery and the remainder was either built over or became part of the Team Valley Trading Estate.

Redheugh House in the mid-nineteenth century.

The Redheugh (meaning 'reed haugh') estate, which occupied most of the area between Bensham and the Tyne, was created by the Redheugh family in the thirteenth and fourteenth centuries, but later passed into the hands of the Askew family after whom Askew Road is named. Industrial developments had a mixed effect on the fortunes of the estate. The construction of the Newcastle & Carlisle Railway through the grounds in the early nineteenth century had an obviously deleterious effect but the opening of the Redheugh Bridge in 1871 with its improved access to Newcastle made it much more attractive as a site for house building.

There were also a number of smaller estates including Derwent Crook, which belonged to the Kepier Hospital in Durham, Deckham Hall which originally belonged to the Dackham family, Field House and Whinney House.

The impact on population

This huge release of building land throughout the nineteenth century had a dramatic effect on the population of the borough, which grew from 8,597 in 1801 (the year of the first official census) to 109,888 in 1901, but for a number of reasons this was not matched by a proportionate increase in the town's wealth.

Firstly, the land released from the break-up of the great estates was relatively inexpensive at a time when many manual workers were being attracted to Tyneside to work in the new labour-intensive industries. The result was the building of large numbers of cheap dwellings to accommodate manual workers, mainly in streets of terraced flats, so that towards the end of the century it was estimated that 95% of Gateshead's working population were wage-earners. As most of the work was in Newcastle, Gateshead became, in effect, a working-class dormitory for Newcastle, a situation which persisted into the twentieth century and provoked J.B. Priestley's 1934 description of Gateshead as 'nothing better than a huge, dingy dormitory' which had been 'carefully planned by an enemy of the human race'.

Secondly, although Gateshead had also benefited from the development of new industry, because this had been mainly concentrated on the Newcastle side of the river, the increase in low-rated residential property was not matched by a corresponding increase in more highly rated industrial property.

Thirdly, the new Council which had come into existence in 1835 was dominated by the so-called 'shopocracy' – local business people – whose main concern was to keep the level of rates low.

All of these factors meant that Gateshead remained a poor authority, a situation which did not change until Government subsidies began to have an effect in the 1930s.

The Great Fire of 1854

The movement of population away from the old riverside area of Gateshead received a tragic additional impetus in 1854 when a great fire occurred which destroyed much of the property in Hillgate. It apparently began in a textile factory in Hillgate, and was first noticed by a policeman on the other side of the river shortly after midnight on the morning of Friday 6 October. Fire-fighting arrangements were still fairly primitive at the time, and despite all available fire-fighting equipment being brought to the site and many volunteers adding their help, the fire continued to burn intensely. Unfortunately, there was a large warehouse containing a number of readily combustible chemicals close to the original seat of the fire, and this warehouse also caught fire, the chemicals apparently generating one or two small explosions which helped to spread the fire to other nearby buildings.

Shortly after 3 a.m., there was an enormous explosion which destroyed the warehouse and scattered burning timber and chemicals over a radius of half a mile or more, causing serious damage to the nearby St Mary's Church, and spreading the fire to Newcastle on the other side of the river. Horse-drawn fire engines were now brought in from all over the northern counties, some from as far away as Berwick to the north and Carlisle to the west, but the fire continued to spread in Gateshead until finally army personnel and miners were brought in to blow up buildings in the path of the fire.

In addition to the enormous damage to industrial property, estimated to be in excess of half a million pounds (equivalent to more than £10 million today), more than fifty people were killed and 200 mainly poor families were made homeless. St Mary's Church was so badly damaged that it was originally proposed to demolish the remains and build a completely new church, but moral and financial support from the general public for retaining the existing church was so great that it was reopened a year later after almost complete rebuilding.

Trade unions

Contrary to what might be expected of a poor, largely working-class population, nineteenth-century Gateshead seems never to have been a strong centre for militant trade union activity, apart from the pitmen whose early struggles are

Chopwell miners' leaders in 1926, the year of the General Strike. From left to right: Jack Lawther, Will Lawther, Steve Lawther, John Gilliland, Ned Wilson, John Stevenson, Eddie Lawther. Will Lawther later became National President of the NUM.

described in a later section about Thomas Hepburn, the early miners' leader. There were, of course, industrial disputes from time to time, but relationships between employers and workers seem to have been fairly amicable until the engineers' 1871 strike in support of a nine-hour day, which lasted from May until October and, although successful, was followed by a series of smaller strikes the following year.

Apart from the miners and the engineers, the other main trade unions were, as might be expected in a railway town, those associated with the railways, where there were stoppages in 1897 and again in 1912. The latter strike was about a false allegation of drunkenness which aroused such strong feelings that the strike spread throughout the region and lasted from October until December.

The influence of the trade unions, notably the engineers and railwaymen, became much stronger in the twentieth century, and was reflected by the total support for the General Strike in 1926, co-ordinated by the Gateshead Trades Council, and their strong representation among members of the former Gateshead Borough Council.

Shopping

As in many industrial towns, the occupiers of the new terraced houses of Gateshead tended to buy their day-to-day needs from small local shops and at one time there seemed to be a shop on almost every street corner. These were often run on a shoestring, with the wife looking after both family and shop during the day while her husband was at work, and both of them looking after the shop in the evenings.

Although the growth in the number of these small corner shops matched the growth in population in the nineteenth century, there was not a corresponding growth in larger-scale shopping facilities in the central area. This was essentially because of the existence of the large shopping area in central Newcastle which was only a short distance away, especially when using one of the bridges at bank-top level which were built from the mid-nineteenth century onwards. Newcastle also offered a vastly greater range of products at competitive prices than the much smaller Gateshead was able to supply. In consequence, shops in Gateshead's High Street have always struggled to offer some competition to their rivals to the north. Although in recent years supermarkets and a new central shopping precinct (albeit with an ugly multi-storey car park attached) have had some success, the town centre has rarely been able to support more than one department store of any size for long.

Snowball's department store was an exception for nearly a century. It was founded in 1850 and occupied a prominent position in the High Street from which it offered a wide range of household goods and furnishings. Unfortunately, the extensive demolition which took place to provide access to the new Tyne Bridge in the 1920s meant that the shop lost its High Street frontage, and although it struggled on for a time, the store finally closed down during the Second World War.

below Old High Street shops in 1911.

following pages The tallest building on the right is Snowball's High Street frontage before it was demolished in the 1920s.

Shepherd's was another department store, which was founded in 1906 and eventually occupied a site in West Street. The store was destroyed by fire in 1946 and although it was rebuilt and re-opened in 1951, it struggled to survive and eventually had to close permanently. The site is now used as a car park for the adjoining branch of Tesco.

above Shephard's store in the 1930s.

left Gateshead Co-operative Society's store in 1962.

The one success story in this field has been the Co-operative Society, which has operated in the town since 1861, moving to its present premises in Jackson Street in 1884. In addition to the Society's large central premises, there are also branches scattered throughout the modern borough, many of which were formerly parts of independent co-operative societies now all merged into the North Eastern Co-operative Society.

It could be said with some justice that a new era began in 1986 with the opening in the west of the borough of the Gateshead Metro Centre, at the time the largest out-of-town shopping complex in Europe. This restored 115 acres of semi-derelict land to productive use with 300 shops occupying 1½ million square feet of shopping space, an eleven-screen cinema, an indoor theme park, fifty eating places and a bowling centre. The centre attracts overseas customers as well as those from all over the United Kingdom, and provides employment for 5,500 local people. At the time of writing (2003) an £85 million development scheme is under way which will add an extra 371,000 square feet of retail space.

chapter five

Getting about

Highways

The growth of population led to major changes in ways of getting about. These days we are so accustomed to ease of travel, with cars, buses, trains and planes to take us to wherever we wish to go, and even without these facilities, good roads on which to walk, that it is sometimes difficult to visualise a time when travel was difficult and dangerous. Good major roads certainly existed in Roman times – in Gateshead, for example, the one which ran from the south across Gateshead Fell and down what became Bottle Bank to the Tyne – but after the Romans left Britain, while much of the road network which they had created remained in use, the road surfaces rapidly fell into disrepair and it was a thousand years before serious efforts were made to create an adequate system of good-quality roads. In any case, relatively few people travelled far from their homes in the Middle Ages, and travellers and traders tended to use horses and pack-horses rather than wheeled vehicles.

Attempts to improve this situation began in the late Middle Ages and an Act passed in 1555 required parishes to appoint Surveyors of Highways who could requisition residents with the necessary resources to work on the roads for four days each year. As may be imagined, this was an unpopular arrange-ment and was rarely enforced with any vigour. It did, however, remain in force until the mid-nineteenth century. In Gateshead, as elsewhere, the Act was implemented with little enthusiasm, although the Surveyors of Highways took over new roads as they were developed. Significant developments included the construction of Jackson Chare/Street (formerly Collier Chare) in 1652, and Church Street (formerly known as George Street or 'the New Street') which was built as a bypass to the very steep Bottle Bank in the late eighteenth century.

The development of increased trade and coach travel between towns led to the introduction of turnpike trusts during the eighteenth century. These trusts were formed to undertake road maintenance which was paid for from tolls levied on travellers. Three such trusts were in operation in Gateshead by the end of the eighteenth century covering the main north/south route (now the Old Durham Road), the road west to Hexham (Jackson Street, Walker Terrace, Bensham Road, High Teams, Lobley Hill, Whickham) and the road east to Sunderland (Sunderland Road).

These turnpike roads tended to follow routes which had been in use for centuries without much regard to the requirements of the increasing volume of wheeled traffic. The north/south road (which later became the old A1), for example, came over the top of Gateshead Fell, probably because the Romans preferred to follow the high ground through hostile terrain. In consequence, it involved a steep bank at the south end (Long Bank) and another steep bank at the north end (Sheriff's Highway – formerly Sodhouse Bank). In 1827, these two banks were bypassed by opening a 'New Durham Road' through Low Fell.

By the mid-nineteenth century, the growing town had acquired its own Council, and this, coupled with a general dissatisfaction with the poor quality of road maintenance and the irritation caused by toll bars, led to the demise of the turnpike trusts. These had all been phased out by 1871, when all highway construction and maintenance became the responsibility of the Town Council.

Later, in the twentieth century, main roads through the town were re-routed and reconstructed as dual carriageways, the old road to Sunderland being replaced by a 'Felling bypass', and the A1, the Great North Road of old, being replaced initially by an eastward diversion to a tunnel under the Tyne at Jarrow and later by a 'Western bypass' to a new bridge over the Tyne at Blaydon.

Public transport

By the end of the eighteenth century, with the gradual improvement in roads, regular stage-coaches were running between Newcastle, London and other major centres, most of them passing through Gateshead, although there was only one major coaching inn in Gateshead, at the Black Bull in the High Street. Gateshead was also linked with other places throughout the North East by a system of carriers who carried both goods and passengers.

Transport within the town itself, however, remained a notable absence until the early years of the nineteenth century when a hackney carriage service was introduced, although this was beyond the means of most working people. A more recognisable approach to public transport began in 1860, when a small number of horse omnibus services were introduced, and horse-drawn vehicles continued to operate across the High Level Bridge (the 'Ha'penny Lop') until 1931. However, a proposal to introduce horse-drawn trams in 1879 was not proceeded with because it was realised that steep inclines within the town would limit their use. Instead, a steam-hauled tramway was finally introduced in the early 1880s, although only three routes were actually completed, to Heworth, Teams and Low Fell.

top A horse-drawn brake which provided an early service across the High Level Bridge.

right A steam tram in the High Street in 1900.

below A tram in Coatsworth Road.

Success with a tramway system finally came towards the end of the century when British Electric Traction Ltd acquired the steam-hauled tramcars, converted them to electric traction and substantially extended the system. This remained the situation until the early 1950s when the tramways were finally phased out to be replaced by buses.

opposite above A bus in
Sheriff's Highway (formerly
Sodhouse Bank), *c.* 1955.

opposite below Competition.
Bus versus tram outside
St Mary's Church, Heworth,
c. 1924.

above Partnership. A
combined bus and tram
waiting room in Low Fell,
c. 1920.

Railways

From a railwayman's point of view, Gateshead could be said to have been a
railway town for many years, with the Greenesfield locomotive works and sheds
and Park Lane sheds providing employment to many local people. Indeed, as
already mentioned, a hundred years ago the North Eastern Railway was the
largest employer in the town. From a passenger's point of view, however,
Gateshead, in this as in so many other ways, was always overshadowed by its
rival on the other side of the Tyne.

Initially, the construction of railways in the region was concerned with
developing east/west routes rather than with routes to the north and south.
Discussions about a link between Tyneside and Carlisle dated from as far
back as 1824 when the option of a canal through the Tyne Gap was considered
but rejected on the grounds of cost. Once the decision to build a railway link
had been agreed, the Newcastle & Carlisle Railway Company finally began
construction in 1830. The first stage, between Hexham and Blaydon, opened in
March 1835, and the whole route from Carlisle as far as Redheugh was opened
in 1838 with passengers for Newcastle completing their journey by ferry.

The official opening took place on 18 June 1838, when thirteen trains travelled
from Redheugh to Carlisle and back. Events on the day might almost have served
as the basis for a stage farce. About a dozen people fell into the river when a
gangway collapsed; because of mistakes in the ticket/seat numbering arrangements tickets could not be linked to appropriate seats, and in consequence
Gateshead councillors, who had arrived first, were properly seated, but other
dignitaries had to hunt for seats, the Lord Mayor of Newcastle ending up on a
plank seat in an open car; the return journey began in a thunderstorm and one
of the carriages was struck by lightning; finally, there were two collisions, one of

Gateshead once had two adjacent stations. This is Gateshead West Station which closed in 1965. Gateshead East Station remained open until it was superseded by the Metro Station in 1981.

which derailed several carriages and injured two passengers causing so much delay that the return journey was not completed until the following morning.

The importance of Redheugh Station (on the Gateshead side of the river) as the eastern terminus of the line did not last long. The Scotswood Railway Bridge was completed in 1839 giving direct access to Newcastle.

There were a number of competing proposals to build a line eastwards from Gateshead including, naturally enough, one from the Newcastle & Carlisle Railway which wanted to extend their existing line as far as Hebburn on the east side of Gateshead. Other groups wanted to build shorter lines linking Blaydon with Friar's Goose, or longer lines as far as South Shields. In the event, after numerous disputes and discussions between the various interested parties, a group called the Brandling Junction Railway Company, which wished to build a line linking Gateshead, South Shields and Monkwearmouth, began construction work in 1836, the first section, through central Gateshead, opening in 1839. Because of the gradients involved, the western incline up from Redheugh was operated with a stationary steam engine, and the line down to a quay at the eastern end of Hillgate was operated as a self-acting incline. In the centre of Gateshead there was a station at Oakwellgate and a viaduct across the High Street which still stands today as an unattractive 'gateway' into Gateshead from the Tyne Bridge.

The same company also relaid the Tanfield Wagonway, albeit still with stationary steam engines and self-acting inclines as well as locomotives, and linked it to the new east/west line, even operating a passenger service on it for a short time. Sadly, the company proved to be over-extended and got into financial difficulties with the result that it passed into the hands of George Hudson, the 'Railway King', in 1844.

The first north/south route was also completed in 1844, by one of George Hudson's companies, the Newcastle & Darlington Joint Railway Company (which became the York & Newcastle Railway Company in 1846). This used the Brandling Junction Railway line at its Gateshead end and terminated in Gateshead so that, having lost one terminus (Redheugh) in 1844, Gateshead acquired another in the same year and on this occasion retained it for five years until the High Level

Bridge making the final connection to Newcastle opened in 1849. The completion of the route from London to Gateshead in 1844 was marked by a train carrying the London morning papers undertaking the full journey which took eight hours, eleven minutes – an average speed of 37mph. In 1868, the North Eastern Railway, which had taken over most of the lines, opened a new north/south line between Durham and Gateshead along the Team Valley, which is virtually the same line as that followed by the main line today.

Although Gateshead lost its last claim to be a railway terminus in 1849, the NER began to enlarge its Greenesfield workshops in 1854, and it is this which gave Gateshead its right to be called a 'railway town'.

The routes which the railways were forced to follow through Gateshead made several estates unsuitable to be the 'residence of a gentleman', as was said of the Redheugh estate in particular, and was undoubtedly a contributory factor to

right A tram beneath the railway bridge in Wellington Street in 1949.

below The southern end of the High Level Bridge with trams at ground level and the railway in the covered section above the arches, *c*. 1924.

the breaking up of the great estates. If the terrain had been different, the railways would have been routed through working-class areas, as happened in other parts of the country. Although this caused great hardship to the residents wherever it occurred, it did at least clear away a great deal of slum property. In Gateshead, this sort of property survived in the Bottle Bank area until it was finally swept away during the building of the Tyne Bridge.

Since the Second World War, an integrated transport system has been developed around a modernised metro railway system. This initially linked Newcastle and Gateshead with the coastal resorts to the east and the airport to the west, and has more recently been extended to the Sunderland area. The Gateshead Interchange Centre which combines Gateshead Metro station with a central bus station and shopping centre, is currently being refurbished.

Bridges

Between Gateshead and Newcastle, the Tyne runs through a gorge 100 feet deep with steep slopes on either side, and for centuries the two towns were

above Old Scotswood Bridge in around 1910; it was demolished in 1967.

below New Scotswood Bridge in 1967.

left Buildings on the medieval bridge.

right The medieval Tyne Bridge.

joined by a single bridge at river level, although ferries and bridges existed further upstream in places which are now part of modern Gateshead, notably at Blaydon and Ryton.

The original bridge was Roman, built in the time of Hadrian, and probably consisted of a wooden platform resting on stone piers. This stayed in use, presumably with some repairs and partial rebuilding work from time to time, until 1248 when it was destroyed by fire. It was replaced in 1250 with a stone bridge, jointly funded by Newcastle and the Bishop of Durham, which became a bone of contention between the two sides for centuries, as described in chapter 1. This bridge was a very substantial structure, carrying not only the roadway across the river, but houses, shops and a chapel, with towers at each end and one in the middle. It was perhaps its sheer bulk that led to its being swept away in 1771 by freak floods down the Tyne valley. On this occasion, however, it took ten years to construct a successor, during which time a wooden bridge and a ferry served as temporary replacements. Despite this long gestation period, the new bridge was less than satisfactory, having to be widened in 1810.

The 1781 Tyne Bridge.

above The Swing Bridge with the High Level Bridge behind, *c.* 1900.

left The High Level Bridge in 1848.

The design also prevented the passage of vessels larger than keels upriver to the growing industry in that area and its foundations were undermined by dredging undertaken by the Tyne Improvement Commission after its establishment in 1850. In consequence, it was decided to replace the bridge yet again, this time with a swing bridge which could open to let vessels through.

The construction of the Swing Bridge began in 1868 and it eventually opened in 1876, at which time it was the largest swing bridge in the world. During its construction a temporary bridge had again to be brought into use. The Swing

Bridge still remains in use today, on the site of the original Roman bridge built nearly 2,000 years ago.

While these changes were taking place at the site of the original river crossing, two other bridges had been built nearby. The possibility of building a bridge level with the tops of the banks on either side of the river, a 'high level' bridge, had been under discussion since the late eighteenth century because of the growing volume of cross-river traffic and the huge inconvenience of moving vehicles and freight up and down the steep banks.

The arrival of the railways turned a desirable project into an absolute necessity and discussion turned to the question of alternative sites. When the views of George Stephenson were sought, he recommended a site to the west of the Swing Bridge and agreed to serve on the joint management committee together with George Hudson, Robert Stephenson serving as consulting engineer. The design eventually agreed upon was an interesting one, consisting of an upper rail bridge over a lower road bridge. Hawks, Crawshay, the firm of which George Hawks, the first Mayor of Gateshead, was senior partner, were contracted to produce the ironwork. Construction began in 1845 and was completed in 1849 when Queen Victoria carried out the opening ceremony. The bridge is still in use today and stands as a striking monument to both the Stephensons and George Hawks.

In this case, many families were displaced by the construction work (130 in Gateshead and many more in Newcastle) but happily, despite the necessity for work to be done at a considerable height above the river, there were no serious accidents.

A third bridge, the Redheugh (road) Bridge, was built further upriver between 1868 and 1871. The engineer in this case was Thomas Bouch who later built the Tay railway bridge which failed so spectacularly. While the Redheugh Bridge did not

The 1871 Redheugh Bridge in around 1895.

reach such a disastrous end, it required constant repairs and was almost completely rebuilt at the end of the nineteenth century. A completely new Redheugh Bridge was opened by Princess Diana in 1983 and the old one demolished.

The fourth bridge to be built was originally called the New High Level Bridge until it was opened by King Edward VII in 1906 when it became known as the King Edward Bridge. This is purely a railway bridge constructed to improve the flow of trains in and out of Newcastle Central Station.

opposite above The 1871 Redheugh Bridge after rebuilding in 1897/1901.

opposite below The modern Tyne Bridge under construction in 1928.

above A tram on the Tyne Bridge in 1938.

The fifth (road) bridge, which completed Tyneside's famous 'Five Bridges', was for many years the most famous Tyne bridge and appropriately enough is known as *the* Tyne Bridge. It was built as a joint project by Gateshead and Newcastle Councils to deal with the congestion caused by increasing volumes of traffic, especially motor traffic, with which the High Level Bridge and the Swing Bridge were struggling to cope. The design of the High Level Bridge was such that it could not be widened, and the Swing Bridge at that time was frequently closed to road traffic to let river traffic through.

Work on the new bridge began in 1923 and was completed in 1928 when it was opened by King George V. As with the High Level Bridge, a great deal of property, mainly slum property, was demolished, leaving people homeless, and some good houses were also destroyed.

While the Swing Bridge had always been toll-free, both the High Level Bridge and the Redheugh Bridge were subject to tolls. The new Tyne Bridge was also made toll-free, after which a campaign began to make all the bridges toll-free, which was finally successful in 1937.

In recent years, the original five bridges have been joined by two others: the Queen Elizabeth Bridge, carrying the line of the Tyneside Metro over the river, and the spectacular Gateshead Millennium 'blinking eye' Bridge which was officially opened by the Queen in 2002. The Millennium Bridge is a revolutionary design – the first of its kind in the world – and is already a tourist attraction which has earned much praise for its engineering.

chapter six

Churches and schools

St Mary's Church

St Mary's Church was historically the parish church of 'old' Gateshead and prior to the nineteenth century was the only Anglican church in Gateshead. Within the modern borough, only two churches can surpass it in longevity – St Mary the Virgin in Whickham, part of which is of Norman origin dating back to the early twelfth century, and Holy Cross Church in Ryton which dates from 1220. The boundaries of the County Borough of Gateshead before it merged with other authorities in 1974 to form the modern metropolitan borough were essentially those of the parish church of St Mary's.

There was a church on or near the site of St Mary's in Norman times but this was destroyed by fire at the time of the killing of the first Norman Bishop of Durham as recounted in chapter one. The present building dates largely from the thirteenth century with the tower being added much later in 1740, although the north wall of the chancel is supposed to date from the early twelfth century. The parish room which was attached to the church was known as the Anchorage, from its occupation by a medieval anchoress, and played a major role in the history of the town. The church was severely damaged in 1854 during the Great Fire and was again damaged by fire in 1979, after which it was deconsecrated and left empty until it enjoyed a brief career as a fine art auction showroom. It has recently been used by the Council as a very successful visitor centre, notably in connection with the Gateshead Quays redevelopment. The success of this latest venture led to the Council obtaining funding from the Heritage Lottery Fund in 2003 to purchase the building and its grounds for permanent use as a heritage and tourist information centre.

Other Anglican churches

The growth in population during the nineteenth century, at a time when church-going was a feature of many more people's lives than it is today, led to a process

above St Mary's Church.

right St Mary's Church in 1827 with the Anchorage (destroyed in the Great Fire of 1854) on the right.

of rapid church building. On Old Durham Road, the ancient Chapel of the Hospital of King James was rebuilt in 1810 as St Edmund's Chapel, and in 1837 the ruined Hospital of St Edmund in the High Street was restored and opened as Holy Trinity.

Elsewhere, St John's Church, which was intended to serve people in the Gateshead Fell area, was consecrated in 1825, the first Rector being William Hawks, a cousin of the George Hawks who later became Gateshead's first Mayor, and in Bensham, St Cuthbert's was built in 1846. Over the years, other churches followed (although some have since closed) and the original single parish of St Mary's was sub-divided into smaller parishes.

Throughout the rest of the area of the modern metropolitan borough, other medieval parishes and parts of parishes made up the original boundaries of Birtley (part of the parish of Chester-le-Street until St John's was consecrated in

left Holy Trinity Church in 1894 with Ellison Schools to the left.

below left St John's Church, Gateshead Fell, in 1828.

below right St Cuthbert's Church, Bensham, in 1893.

1849), Felling (a chapelry in the parish of Jarrow St Paul until 1843), Ryton and Blaydon (the parish of Holy Cross), and Whickham (the parish of St Mary the Virgin). These followed similar processes during the nineteenth century as populations grew, and were broken up into numerous smaller parishes.

Methodism

John Wesley was ordained as a Church of England minister in 1728 but became a committed evangelist in 1738 and spent the next fifty years travelling round the country on horseback and preaching to open-air meetings. Initially, Methodism remained within the Church of England and only broke away to become a separate body in 1795. Even after this split, however, relations between 'Church and Chapel' often remained cordial and as late as 1840, for example, one

opposite above Holy Cross Church , Ryton, *c.* 1900.

opposite below St Mary the Virgin, Whickham, in 1921.

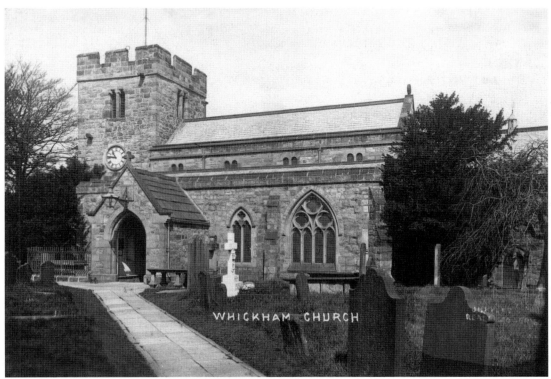

WHICKHAM CHURCH

Chowdene Bank which
Wesley visited in 1743.

Whickham man managed to be both parish clerk in the Church of England and singing master in the Methodist chapel. Even later, the Rector of Whickham presented bibles and testaments to the newly formed Methodist Sunday School.

Wesley's first visit to Gateshead itself was in 1743 when he passed 'a little village called Chowden (sic), which they told me consisted of colliers only. I resolved to preach there as soon as possible, for they are sinners and need repentance'. When he returned to Chowdene shortly afterwards, he encountered 'twenty or thirty wild children' who 'could not be said to be either clothed or naked'.

Methodism made rapid progress in Gateshead and Durham, particularly amongst communities of pitmen like this one, probably because it offered a less formal, more 'down to earth' approach than the established Church, which tended to be seen as the Church of the ruling class, in particular the mine owners. Like most radical movements, however, Methodism began to fragment in the nineteenth century, resulting in the establishment of a large number of churches/chapels, although most of these were fairly small.

The first Methodist chapel to be built in Gateshead was at the junction of High Street and Ellison Street and there is an entertaining story told about its minister in the late 1820s. On one occasion, being disappointed about the very small congregation, he is said to have walked up the High Street as far as Sunderland Road and then run back to the chapel shouting 'A fight, a fight'. Having by this means attracted a large crowd, he then announced: 'Friends, you have come to see a fight, and you will not be disappointed because I am going to have one with the Devil.'

The various strands of Methodism were finally reunited in 1932, since when rationalisation has led to the closure of many churches although Methodism remains a very strong tradition in the area.

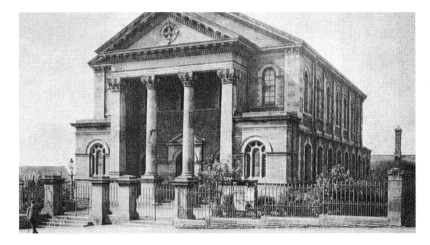

above Competing chapels in a mining area. Wesleyan (on the left) and Primitive (centre) Methodist Chapels at Marley Hill.

right Bensham Road Wesleyan Methodist Chapel, built in 1872.

Roman Catholicism

After the religious struggles of the sixteenth and seventeenth centuries, Roman Catholics tended to keep a low profile in the area, as they did elsewhere, but this seems to have been particularly advisable in Gateshead as there were reports in the sixteenth century contrasting the 'good protestants of Gateshead' with the 'papists' of Newcastle. In the nineteenth century, however, part of the general growth in population consisted of Irish immigrants drawn into the area by the jobs available and this considerably strengthened the Catholic position.

In view of the increased number of Catholics, the Bishop of Hexham and Newcastle decided to appoint a priest in 1850 with a view to forming a Catholic parish. The priest appointed got off to a bad start by announcing that the town

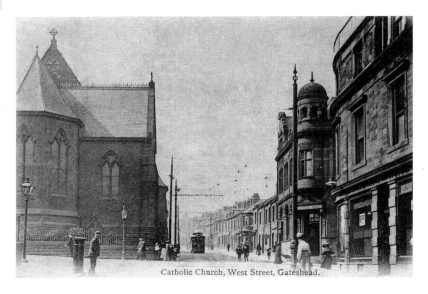

Catholic Church, West Street, Gateshead.

St Joseph's Roman Catholic
Church (on the left) *c.* 1900.

had been 'too long without a church and pastor' and describing himself as
'Parish Priest Elect of Gateshead', which was taken to be a direct attack on the
established Church and caused some acrimony. Fortunately, this soon died
down and a fund-raising campaign (working men paid one shilling (5p) a
month) led to the opening of St Joseph's Church, at the junction of High West
Street and Bensham Road, in 1859. More Roman Catholic churches have since
been built elsewhere in the borough.

Other churches

Other churches and beliefs represented in the modern borough cover a very
wide range and include not only other strands of Christian belief but representatives of, for example, Buddhists, Hindus and Muslims, to name but a few. One
group which deserves special mention, however, is the Jewish community,
which was established in 1887 and remains a fairly small, close-knit community which, despite its small size, has achieved an international reputation as a
centre for Jewish Rabbinical studies.

Anchorage School

As in many other places, the first school in the borough was set up by the
Church and was known as the Anchorage because it was originally held in the
parish room attached to St Mary's Church, which has already been mentioned.
It is not known exactly when the school was founded but it seems to have been
in existence as early as 1628 when the vestry minutes refer to 'lyme for the
schole, 5s 6d' (27½p). This is well before other early schools in the area which
tend to date from the early eighteenth century. In 1657, another minute is more
specific when it refers to 'Mr Jno. Thompson, Minister, who teacheth schole in
the Anchoridge'.

1, 2 In the blink of an eye. Gateshead
Millennium Bridge lowered for pedestrian use
(top) and raised for river traffic (below).

3 *above* Baltic Centre for Contemporary Art from the
Millennium Bridge, 2003.

4 *opposite above* The new Hilton Hotel, 2003.

5 *opposite below* Four of the Tyne bridges. From
the front: Tyne, Swing, High Level and Metro.

6 *above* St Mary's Church, 2003.

7 *left* Clock outside the Town Hall, 2003.

8 *above* The Metropole Hotel on the site of the former Metropole Theatre, later the Scala cinema.

9 *right* Former entrance to Gateshead House, which was destroyed by fire in 1746.

10 *left* St Joseph's Roman Catholic Church, 2003.

11 *below* Regent Terrace opposite the Civic Centre, 2003.

12 *above* Angel of the North.

13 *right* Statue of George Hawks, first Mayor
of Gateshead, on Windmill Hills.

14, 15 Two of the oldest churches in Gateshead –
Whickham's St Mary the Virgin (above) and Ryton's
Holy Cross (right).

A later Rector, Dr Theophilus Pickering, moved the school into the Tollbooth in the High Street which had previously been used, no doubt appropriately in the minds of its scholars, as a lock-up. In his will (he died in 1710), this Rector also endowed the school with £300 and specified that the master (there was only one) should be a poor clergyman who, in addition to the more usual subjects, had to teach Latin, Greek, accounts and navigation – a remarkably talented clergyman was obviously required.

Although the school was essentially a fee-paying institution, there were spaces for fifteen free scholars who were taught grammar, maths and geography. Also, although it was the only school in the borough throughout the eighteenth century, many of the more affluent families sent their children elsewhere to be educated, many to Newcastle but some even further afield (including Eton).

The school seems to have flourished and by the early years of the nineteenth century the staff included two assistants as well as the master, and there were nearly 100 paying pupils. These were taught a range of subjects depending on the fees their parents were prepared to pay, ranging from reading only, which cost 10s 6d (52½p) per quarter, to a comprehensive list which included reading, writing, grammar, arithmetic, accounts, Latin, Greek, geography, the use of globes, history, mathematics and French, costing £1 11s 6d (£1.57½) per quarter.

From the early years of the nineteenth century, however, other schools had started to develop and the Anchorage began to suffer from the comparison – it lacked a playground, for example. The school was renovated in 1876, but when the then master died shortly afterwards, it proved impossible to find a replacement and the school finally closed in 1878, at which time it had been serving the people of Gateshead for more than 250 years.

Other early schools

Many of the schools which were set up in the nineteenth century were also associated with churches and were fee-paying. The first of these appears to have been opened in 1808 in a local inn, but in 1810 moved to the newly rebuilt St Edmund's Chapel and thereafter was known as the 'Chapel' school, although its ethos was Anglican. This accommodated 350 children paying 1d (0.4p) per week and used the 'monitor' system with only two teachers, the younger children being supervised by the older children. Although having the advantage of being very cheap, this was obviously a very poor method of education and an inspector's report in 1851 recorded that the only 'textbook' in use was the bible, and the standard of instruction was very low.

Other Anglican schools were the Ellison Schools which were built next to the Holy Trinity Chapel in the High Street in 1838, and the Lady Vernon Schools which were opened in 1864 and were connected with St Cuthbert's Church. Many of the numerous Methodist chapels also had schools attached to them and a Roman Catholic school was opened next to St Joseph's Church in 1864. One non-denominational school for boys was opened in 1841 but its fees were 3d (1.25p) per week and it closed in 1850.

There were also, of course, a number of private or 'dame' schools which opened from time to time but, like most of their kind, these tended to be very inefficient and did not last long. Of more importance were the schools attached to factories to educate not only the children of their employees, but often the employees themselves, many of whom were also children. Although there appear to be few surviving records of these institutions, they certainly existed among the larger firms such as Hawks Iron Works and the Friar's Goose Chemical Works.

Despite the range of provision which existed, albeit much of it of poor quality, it was estimated in 1842 that of the children aged from five to fifteen in the area of the Gateshead Poor Law Union (roughly the area of the present metropolitan borough) less than a third were attending a school.

above St Mary's National School, established in 1841.

opposite above Windmill Hills Board School.

opposite below Secondary school (later boys' grammar school) built in 1883 by the School Board.

School Board

The situation in Gateshead was not untypical of the situation elsewhere in the country and in 1870 the Government passed the Elementary Education Act authorising the setting up of School Boards to investigate the availability of education in their areas and to make provision to meet any deficiency. Gateshead set up a School Board in the same year, becoming one of the first places nationally to do so.

The census carried out by the new Board in 1871 showed that, of the approximate 8,000 children of school age in Gateshead itself, nearly half were not receiving education of any sort, and the Board decided to build an additional five schools to deal with this unmet demand. This programme was completed in 1879, and thereafter new schools were built at an average rate of one every two years to meet the rapidly growing demand until 1903, when the Board ceased

to exist. During the same period, although it was not its prime purpose, the Board also gradually took over the former church-sponsored schools, so that by the time of its demise the Board was providing more than 80% of the school places available in the borough.

The schools provided by the Board were initially elementary schools, the curriculum being limited to the three Rs plus grammar, geography and needle-work, although religious instruction was also emphasised and, in practice, time was allowed for activities such as drawing and singing as well as practical subjects like cookery. As time went on, the Board also included technical subjects and even modern languages, besides encouraging physical exercise and games, including football and swimming.

Education offices, built for the
School Board in 1897.

Several forerunners of branches of the modern education service were also
initiated by the Board: 'secondary' education in the form of two Higher Grade
Schools, one for boys (which later became the Gateshead Grammar School)
and one for girls; 'further' and 'community' education in the form of evening
classes for working people, not only to further their education but also to allow
them to enjoy recreational activities as well; and 'special' education in the form
of an Industrial School for children at risk.

Private schools continued but increasingly unsuccessfully, and were attacked
in 1876 by the secretary to the Board who claimed that many of them were a
'mere asylum for irregular attenders' and were hindering the work of the Board.

Education Committee

The Education Act of 1902 transferred responsibility for education to local
authority committees, since when education has always been the major element
in local government spending.

Because of the Board's activities, the provision of all-age elementary education was regarded as satisfactory and the new Education Committee therefore
directed its attention to other areas of education. The Committee's activities
were also affected by the rising levels of unemployment, because the education
service was regarded as the natural channel for the distribution of 'welfare'
benefits to deprived children. However, a proposal to provide free school meals
was rejected as 'socialistic', despite having been specifically authorised by the
Provision of Meals Act of 1906. Fortunately this decision was reversed in 1910,
although even then the *Newcastle Evening Chronicle* condemned the decision
to provide free meals as encouraging 'thriftlessness and parental neglect'. For
whatever reason, the quality of school meals was poor from their introduction
and remained so right up to the Second World War, with the result that only
those in direst need took advantage of them.

Another Act, in 1907, made medical inspections compulsory and this service subsequently expanded very considerably with the appointment of a specialist Schools Medical Officer. A Boot and Clog Fund (later the Boot and Shoe Fund) was also operated from the 1920s onward.

During the 1920s and 1930s, the pressing need for improved secondary and technical education in the borough became obvious. The elementary schools established by the Board were all-age institutions attended by the vast majority of children and there were very few secondary school places available until after the Second World War. The one grammar school (former 'Higher Grade' school) which had been co-educational became single-sex when a Girls' Grammar School was built in 1956. This was followed by nine new secondary schools, mainly secondary modern, in the period up to 1967 when it was decided to convert all secondary schools into comprehensive schools. Because of the size and siting of the new secondary schools, the structure decided upon was one of paired Junior and Senior High Schools, and this structure continued until after local government reorganisation when they were gradually converted into single site, all-through comprehensive schools to bring them into line with the schools in the other local authorities involved in the merger (all previously under the control of Durham Education Committee).

Technical education was very sketchy in the borough, and as early as 1909, an inspector concluded that 'the present makeshift policy of the LEA must be condemned'. Despite this, lack of resources meant that the problem persisted throughout the inter-war years, and it was not until the pressing need for trained people became apparent during the Second World War that a Technical Institute was established in Durham Road. This was re-named Gateshead Technical College in 1945 and moved into purpose-built accommodation in 1955 which has since been considerably enlarged. Since then the syllabus has been extended to include, *inter alia*, A-level studies and the college has been re-named Gateshead College.

Bensham Settlement

The Bensham Settlement was set up in 1919 in the former home of Robert Spence Watson, whose life is summarised in chapter 10. Its purpose was to provide educational, social and recreation facilities, at which it was successful, but it relied upon donations for financial support, and financial problems led to its being taken over by the Education Committee in 1948. The first nursery school in Gateshead was set up in Bensham Grove in 1929, and later moved into a purpose-built building in the garden in 1931, but here again donations proved inadequate, and the Council assumed control in 1939.

Metropolitan borough

Since the metropolitan borough came into existence, the education service has seen immense changes. In the primary sector, the Council has followed a policy of combining infant and junior schools into all-through primary schools; replacing older buildings, many of them dating from the Board period and therefore over a century old; and adding nursery provision as fast as Government-spending restrictions have allowed.

In the secondary sector, staying-on rates remained low throughout the borough for many years, with only two schools (marginally) meeting the Government's minimum figure of 150 pupils for a viable sixth form. In the 1980s, a scheme was drawn up to make staying on more attractive to what were, after all, young adults, by concentrating all post-sixteen education at Gateshead College in a new purpose-built building. Unfortunately, Government restrictions on capital spending, the removal of colleges from local authority control and changes in the law relating to school management meant that the scheme had to be abandoned. Despite this, some of the planned benefits have been achieved, partly through the development of close working arrangements between college and schools, and staying-on rates have improved dramatically. The college governors are also planning a new college building in the Gateshead Quays area.

Improvements have also been achieved in special education following a major reorganisation, and in community education where the education service is now responsible for 107 community centres and other community organisations.

chapter seven

Leisure activities

Work and leisure

Until the late nineteenth century most people had very little leisure time. Many workers were working twelve-hour shifts on six days of the week with their only free day being Sunday, when there were pressures to attend church or chapel. Statutory bank holidays were only introduced in the 1870s and the idea of annual holidays lay many years in the future. Breaks did occur, of course, when the pit or workshop was closed, but when this happened there was no money coming in so the enforced 'holidays' were hardly occasions for rejoicing. Even when in work, low pay levels limited what could be done in the small amount of free time available.

In addition to lack of time and money, a further constraint was the absence of public transport on which to travel about to pursue leisure activities. In consequence, these tended to be fairly local in nature.

Pubs and clubs

Public houses represented early answers to these problems. While they were essentially providing beer to customers who were engaged in heavy manual work which was often hot and dusty, they were also local, relatively cheap (provided one did not drink too much) and were available within licensing hours for as long or as short a time as the customer wanted. In consequence, in the absence of any alternative meeting places, the pub also served as an early form of community centre, and many clubs and societies met in the local pub. Pubs also served as venues for meetings of various sorts including election meetings, dinners and music festivals, a tradition continued today with the widespread annual leek shows.

With competition between public houses for custom, pubs also began to offer their own entertainment. Cock-fighting was a popular 'sport' and there were several cockpits attached to public houses in the Gateshead area. More

The Three Tuns on Sodhouse Bank, c. 1910.

acceptably to modern eyes, some pubs evolved into music halls of which there were several in Gateshead, although the most famous, immortalised in 'The Blaydon Races', was Balmbra's across the river in Newcastle. Games like quoits and billiards appeared in many pubs during the early twentieth century, and coach trips to the seaside or even further afield became popular during the inter-war years.

The working men's club movement, surprisingly enough, began not in the North East but in London and was originally largely a temperance movement directed towards mental and moral improvement. Clubs first appeared in Gateshead in the 1870s, and spread rapidly after the original temperance link was abandoned, particularly in the early years of the twentieth century. The club movement was so successful that it built its own brewery, the Federation Brewery, which was originally based in Newcastle but moved to the Gateshead side of the river in 1980/81.

Clubs still form a significant element in social life in the borough although the disappearance of much of the old heavy industry and changing lifestyles have tended to cause financial problems in recent years.

Swalwell Hoppings, c. 1905.

Hoppings

Another form of local activity were the hoppings, a sort of carnival combining a fair, races, competitions and other pastimes held once a year in town and village centres. The hoppings in Gateshead were held on the Windmill Hills but seem to have ceased early in the nineteenth century, whereas the hoppings in Whickham, for example, were held on the village green and lasted until the 1930s.

Among the most famous were the Swalwell Hoppings of the eighteenth and nineteenth centuries, which lasted for a week and attracted people from all over Tyneside. These included horse races, a fairground, shows like Punch and Judy, exhibitions of wild animals, and a variety of competitions, one of which was grinning, now known as 'gurning', for tobacco.

Nowadays, the only hoppings still in existence appear to be the great Annual Hoppings held on Newcastle Town Moor, which are essentially a giant fair.

Rowing

Apart from horse racing, which seems to have had only a short life in Gateshead in the early eighteenth century, rowing was the first great spectator sport on Tyneside. On race days thousands of people lined the riverbanks, and considerable amounts of money were wagered on races over a stretch of the Tyne between the High Level Bridge and Scotswood.

The first great oarsman was Harry Clasper of Dunston, who was not only regarded as champion of the Tyne, but raced on the Thames, the Mersey, the Clyde, Loch Lomond and elsewhere. In addition to his ability in competitive

rowing, he also excelled in boatbuilding, on which he concentrated after retiring from active competition. Interestingly enough, Geordie Ridley, the songwriter, gave the first performance of 'The Blaydon Races' at a testimonial dinner for Harry Clasper in Balmbra's. A fuller account of his life is given in *Whickham History & Guide*.

Clasper was followed as champion by Robert Chambers of Newcastle, but the championship was subsequently brought back to Gateshead by James Renforth, an account of whose life is given later in chapter 10. After Renforth's death in 1871, the championship passed to the Thames, and rowing declined as a spectator sport on Tyneside, although there have been signs of a renewed interest in recent years.

Memorial to Harry Clasper, the great oarsman, in Whickham churchyard.

Athletics and Gateshead International Stadium

In modern times, Gateshead's most important sporting involvement has been in athletics, centred upon Gateshead International Stadium. The stadium was originally opened in 1955 as the Gateshead Youth Stadium, with a cinder track, but after local government reorganisation in 1974 the stadium became an early beneficiary of the Council's support for sporting activities and was upgraded in the same year with a synthetic track on which Brendan Foster proceeded to break the 3,000-metre world record in front of an ecstatic Gateshead crowd. The track was re-surfaced in 1982 and again in 2003 to maintain the stadium's status as a world-class centre for sporting activities. Since Brendan Foster's record-breaking run, the stadium has hosted many national and international events and has entertained many leading international athletes. Brendan Foster has since pursued a successful career as a businessman and sports commentator, but has also sponsored long-distance running events including the hugely successful Great North Run, a half-marathon run mainly through Gateshead and the neighbouring South Tyneside.

The stadium is also well used by members of the general public, in particular by schools and sporting organisations like the Gateshead Harriers and Athletics Club (President: Brendan Foster). Athletics is not, of course, confined to the stadium and there are other athletics centres in the borough, notably in Blaydon with the Blaydon Harriers and Athletics Club.

The stadium nowadays is an all-seater stadium with a capacity of 11,800, and in addition to the outdoor facilities there are excellent indoor facilities for sports such as five-a-side football, basketball, hockey, badminton, indoor tennis, netball and weight training.

Football

Association football has as many passionate supporters in Gateshead as elsewhere, but although the borough has had many excellent amateur teams (Whickham won the FA Vase in 1981) at professional level the vast majority have always supported either Newcastle or Sunderland rather than the town's own team.

Gateshead Football Club's former ground at Redheugh Park.

The latter, which claims to be the senior non-league club in the North East, has had a complicated history. Not only was the club founded when the former

South Shields moved to the Gateshead Redheugh Park ground in 1930 and became Gateshead AFC, but history repeated itself in 1975 when a later South Shields club again moved to the town to become Gateshead United, playing at the Gateshead International Stadium where the present team still plays.

The stadium is also home to Gateshead Thunder RLFC, the Rugby League Club, and the Gateshead International Senators (GIs), the longest established and most successful team playing American football in the North East.

above Gateshead Football Club in 1960.

opposite Traditional entertainment in the North East. Winlaton Rapper Clog Dancers.

Other sports

It is not possible in a short general history to give a comprehensive account of the evolution of all the sporting activity in the borough, but many clubs have histories dating back a hundred years or more. Among those which are still active, excluding those associated with schools, there are seven cricket teams, six golf clubs, four rugby clubs, three amateur football clubs and three bowling clubs. There are also, of course, swimming pools, tennis courts, squash courts, riding schools and the like, and as well as a variety of leisure centres, activity centres and sports halls, there is also a Water Sports Club based at Friar's Goose.

It's a Knockout

On a lighter note, Gateshead performed extremely well when competing in the television programme *It's a Knockout* in 1980, beating both Newcastle and Sunderland. The team went on to compete in the final in Coburg, Germany, but sadly failed to win. Although these competitions made entertaining and often amusing television, anyone who observed the 'games' close up will be aware of the considerable physical demands made on contestants, and the hard work and determination needed to compete successfully.

Open spaces

Over the years, the six local authorities which came together in 1974 to form the modern borough have created a total of twenty-nine parks and open spaces, including Chopwell and Washingwell Woods which now form part of the Great North Forest. In 1962, the closure of the Derwent branch line meant that the line could be converted into the very pleasant Derwent Walk through what is now attractive countryside. More recently, the clearance of the Watergate Colliery and Derwenthaugh Coke Works sites have given the Council the opportunity to turn them into large, attractive parkland spaces open to the general public.

Although each of these open spaces is worthy of note, by far the largest and finest park, not only in the borough but possibly in the north of England, is Saltwell Park.

Saltwell Park

The former County Borough of Gateshead began considering the provision of a public park in the late 1850s, and the first park was actually opened on Windmill Hills in 1861. The original intention was to enlarge this by purchasing additional land, but the cost proved prohibitive, and no further action was taken for some years.

In 1875, the Council purchased an estate in Saltwell from William Wailes, a local stained-glass manufacturer. This comprised four fields totalling 52 acres together with Saltwell Towers, a striking mansion house which had been built for William Wailes in 1862. Edward Kemp, who had designed Birkenhead Park, which subsequently served as a model for New York's Central Park, was

above Saltwell West Park Bowling Club, *c.* 1917.

opposite above The lake in Saltwell Park, *c.* 1910.

opposite below The Dene in Saltwell Park, *c.* 1900.

commissioned to prepare a ground plan which is reflected in the shape of the park today. This entailed removing the existing hedges, creating a main entrance from the town at the north-east corner which opened onto a broad walk along the east side of the park, and providing facilities for bowling, skating and croquet together with a refreshment room and drinking fountain. Typically for the time, the borough surveyor also ordered a dozen 'keep off the grass' notices.

The park opened in 1876 but numerous improvements were made over the following decade. The first bandstand was erected in 1876 but thereafter was

moved to a variety of different locations as the park developed. A menagerie was added in 1877, a lake, an aviary and a monkey-house in 1880, facilities for tennis in 1884 and for quoits in 1886.

In the twentieth century, the park was substantially enlarged with the addition of the Saltwell Grove estate in 1920, and the adaptation of Saltwell Towers to serve as a museum in 1933 – a use which was sadly ended by the discovery of dry rot in 1969.

The park has been a great asset to the town throughout its history, being well used by successive generations as a recreational area and as a focal point for the celebration of national and local events. It also played a significant role during the Second World War when many successful activities were held in the park in support of the 'Holidays at Home' movement, and a substantial under-ground air-raid shelter was built there.

At the time of writing (2003), Gateshead Council is engaged on a major overhaul and renewal exercise which will see the park reinvigorated and ready to face the demands of the next century or so.

Libraries

There were no public libraries in Gateshead throughout most of the nineteenth century, despite the formation of the new Borough Council in 1835, because of concerns about the potential 'burden on the rates'.

The first library in the town was that available to members of the Mechanics Institute, which was founded in 1836 by a number of leading citizens. The Institute was originally intended to offer members of the working class facili-ties for 'self-improvement' through the provision of a library and a programme of lectures. Some years later, however, it was pointed out that it was used

Gateshead Central Library
before enlargement, c. 1933.

by every class in the community except the mechanics for whom it was intended.

Initially, meetings were held in the Town Hall and various other locations, but the number of members never rose much above 250. In 1844 it was decided that what the Institute needed was a permanent building and a purpose-built building was opened in West Street in 1848. As the century progressed, however, other groups concerned with self-improvement began to develop. Many of these were originally church-based, like the Gateshead Mutual Improvement Society which grew out of St Mary's Sunday School in 1860, while others were work-based like the North Eastern Railway Literary Institute, which had a library of over 12,000 books and ran science and art classes.

For whatever reason, the new Institute building did not have the desired effect of increasing the numbers of members, but the trustees struggled on, even fending off a proposal in 1881 to convert it into a free public library because of the effect on the rates. Instead, in the same year, they agreed to merge with the Gateshead Mutual Improvement Society mentioned above, which had the effect of increasing its membership to over 500 but diluted its original objectives to the extent that it gradually became little more than a middle-class social club.

The opposition of the Mechanics Institute trustees to becoming a publicly funded body resulted in the public library issue being debated by the burgesses which led eventually, to a narrow vote in favour of setting up a public library. The new library building, in Swinburne Street, was opened in 1885, and was so successful that twenty years later moves began to develop bigger premises in Prince Consort Road which were finally opened in 1926. This building continues in use, although considerably enlarged, as the Central Library with, to date, a total of sixteen branch libraries spread throughout the present borough offering not only books but a wide range of other services also.

Shipley Art Gallery

above Shipley Art Gallery, built in 1915.

The town owes its art gallery to the generosity of J.A.D. Shipley, a local resident who died in 1909 and left his collection of paintings and the sum of £30,000 to build a gallery to house them. Although Shipley lived in Gateshead, indeed, in the Saltwell Towers mentioned previously, he had worked as a solicitor in Newcastle, and Newcastle was his first choice to be the recipient of his generosity with Gateshead as reserve. The gift was not an unmixed blessing. There were 2,500 paintings, some of doubtful value, and the size of the collection would have necessitated the construction of a very large building indeed (larger than the Louvre, it was suggested). Fortunately for Gateshead, Newcastle, which already had the Laing Art Gallery, decided against accepting the bequest leaving Gateshead as the beneficiary. After having the pictures assessed, Gateshead sold half of them and used the money, together with the original £30,000, to build the Shipley Art Gallery. Building was begun in 1914 and the gallery was opened in 1917, since when it has been a constantly improving asset to the town.

Museum

The absence of a museum in the town remains a notable lack. Interestingly, Shipley's former home, Saltwell Towers, was acquired for this purpose by the Council in 1932, at which time the building was empty and semi-derelict. After thirty-seven years of use as a local and industrial museum, dry rot forced its closure in 1969. The building is now being renovated as part of the redevelopment of Saltwell Park. As mentioned in the previous chapter, the Council has now acquired St Mary's Church for use as a heritage and tourist information centre.

left Essoldo Cinema in 1968.

right The Little Theatre in 1966.

Music, theatres and cinemas

As has already been mentioned, music halls were originally adjuncts to public houses and more serious theatre, in the form of travelling troupes, initially used the same venues. Later, permanent theatres were built, notably the Theatre Royal (later renamed the Queens), Metropole, Standard and King's (later the Empire). When cinemas arrived in the early twentieth century they initially operated out of converted shops, then gradually took over the theatres, sometimes offering extra entertainment like live stage acts, theatre organs, or even full orchestras. Finally, the era of the purpose-built cinema arrived but, by the 1950s, the cinema was already in decline, overtaken by television, although some of the cinema buildings survived for a time as bingo halls.

In the non-professional field, the Gateshead area has always supported a wide range of musical and theatrical groups including amateur dramatic, operatic and choral societies as well as more traditional northern activities like male voice choirs and brass bands, but the lack of suitable halls has meant that over the years these have tended to migrate to the other side of the river, a tendency which it is to be hoped the Gateshead Quays developments will now reverse.

Meantime, one outstanding exception has been the famous Felling Male Voice Choir, which was founded in 1920 and regularly performs across the northern region, and even farther afield on occasion, while still retaining its base in Felling. Another 1920 survivor has been the Gateshead Little Theatre, which had its origins as a drama group associated with the Independent Labour Party, but has since evolved into the (non-political) Little Theatre of today.

chapter eight

Local government

St Mary's Church

In the past, churches played a much more active role in society than they do today, and what we now regard as functions of local government were usually carried out by officers of the local church, which was therefore not only the focus of religious life in the community but the administrative centre also. This history is still reflected in local government today because although the Municipal Corporations Act of 1835 created the structure of modern local government, local Council boundaries can still be traced back to the boundaries of the old Church of England parishes before these were sub-divided in the nineteenth century to reflect the growth in population. In Whickham, for example, the boundaries of the old Whickham Urban District Council followed the boundaries of the original parish of St Mary the Virgin before it was sub-divided into the four modern parishes. Similarly, the boundaries of the area covered by Blaydon and Ryton Urban District Councils followed the old bound-aries of the parish of Holy Cross which originally incorporated both areas.

The boundaries of 'old' Gateshead reflect the boundaries of the original parish of St Mary's, which played a central part in the life of the community in many different ways, although other bodies gradually came to play an impor-tant role in local affairs.

The 'four and twenty'

In most parts of the country there were annual meetings of parishioners ('open' vestries) to elect church wardens and other parish officers, but in the North East, for reasons lost in the past, a less democratic system developed whereby these appointments were made by 'select' vestries. These consisted of a speci-fied number of parishioners (often 'four and twenty', hence the popular name), usually the more affluent members of the community, who were self-appointing and served for life.

In Gateshead there are no surviving minutes of meetings of the 'four and twenty' prior to 1626, but they seem to have been in existence well before that date and continued to function as an administrative body throughout the seventeenth and eighteenth centuries. They levied rates for the maintenance of the poor, for church repairs and other purposes and appointed a range of parish officials including overseers of the poor, overseers of the highways, constables, grassmen (who looked after the common fields) and, at one stage, wainmen (who collected dues from wains passing through the town).

The powers of the 'four and twenty' declined progressively over the years, partly as competing groups emerged in the town and partly as the result of Government legislation. Oddly enough, in the submissions made by Gateshead during its struggle against annexation by Newcastle, the 'four and twenty' were not mentioned as part of the government of Gateshead. The address sent to the Speaker of the House of Commons in 1576, for example, states that:

> The town of Gateshead is ruled by bailiff and burgesses and hath good and wholesome constitutions and ordinances within themselves, and is as well governed for justice as they are in Newcastle.

This group of people obviously played an equally important role in local affairs.

Bailiff and burgesses (borough-holders)

The Bailiff was appointed by the Bishop as his chief agent in the town, usually from amongst the local landed gentry. One of the Bailiff's main functions was to collect the town's revenues from, for example, farming rents, fisheries, mills and tolls of various sorts. The financial arrangements with the Bishop varied from one whereby the Bailiff kept the proceeds in return for an annual payment to the Bishop to a later system whereby the Bailiff passed the proceeds on in return for an annual salary. The Bailiff had a staff of executive officers to carry out his various functions including a steward responsible for day-to-day administration and, interestingly, a town wait who played the pipes at the mowing of the town fields.

The burgesses, or borough-holders, were the holders of certain specific properties in the old town centre. They were obliged to attend meetings of the borough court, which usually met once a fortnight and was responsible for making bye-laws for the management of the town, but in return enjoyed a share in the town fields and freedom from tolls. Because these rights as a borough-holder were not hereditary but passed with the property, which could be subdivided, the number of borough-holders fluctuated and by the early eighteenth century had reached a figure of 130.

The date when this system was introduced is unknown but records show that a Bailiff was in post as early as the thirteenth century, and it carried on with little modification until the sixteenth century. The potential for conflict from time to time between the Bailiff, borough-holders and the 'four and twenty' is obvious, and particularly so during the period of the Grand Lease between 1581 and 1679, when the borough court was controlled by Newcastle which also appointed the Bailiff.

Lords of the manor

Shortly after the Bishop regained control of the town in 1684, he made radical changes in the way it was governed. In place of a Bailiff, the twin manors of Gateshead and Whickham were leased to a lord of the manor who received all the income generated from the two manors in return for an annual rental.

The first lords of the manor under this arrangement were all absentee land-lords leaving the management of the two manors to a resident steward, resulting in a significant deterioration in the land. In 1716, however, William Cotesworth became lord of the manor on the death of his brother-in-law, William Ramsay, and set about improving the estate. Sadly, his expenditure on this project, and on a number of lawsuits defending the manors, put him into financial difficulties by the time of his death in 1726. His son, Robert, resolved the problem by separating the two manors and selling off Whickham, which thereafter had an independent history (as recounted in *Whickham History & Guide*) until the two were reunited in the new metropolitan borough in 1974.

After Robert's death in 1728 the manor of Gateshead eventually came into the hands of the Carr and Ellison families, who provided lords of the manor until 1857 when the lordship passed into the hands of the Ecclesiastical Commissioners who were empowered to sell off the remaining manorial land. The lordship finally ceased in 1924.

Freemen

The freemen were yet another group who took part in the governance of the town. They were members of the various trade guilds which had grown up since the sixteenth century, at least partly as a defence against similar bodies in Newcastle who tried to extend their monopoly practices into Gateshead. Freemen covered a wide range of trades, some in guilds for a single trade such as glovers and weavers, and others covering a mixture of trades. The first such 'composite' guild, for example, covered dyers, fullers, blacksmiths, locksmiths, cutlers, joiners and carpenters.

By the middle of the seventeenth century, the freemen had by some means secured a major role in relation to the town's common lands in Bensham and on Gateshead Fell. Pasture rights over these had once belonged to the community as a whole but in 1647 a parliamentary survey stated that they belonged to 'the free borough men and freemen of the said manor of Gateshead' and in 1652 the 'four and twenty' issued an instruction that cattle should not be grazed on Gateshead Fell unless they 'really belong to the borough men or freemen of this corporation'. These were very interesting statements for a number of reasons. Firstly, they made it clear that the formerly common fields had mysteriously become private property; secondly, the freemen had somehow become equal partners with the borough-holders; and thirdly, they revealed the confused state of administration where the 'four and twenty' were issuing instructions about the town fields although these were now supposed to be effectively under the control of the borough-holders and freemen. This last issue was finally sorted out in 1695 when the borough-holders appointed two stewards to oversee the town fields and assumed responsibility for the four grassmen. Throughout the eighteenth century, control of Gateshead Fell, however, remained a subject of constant friction between the borough-holders and freemen on the one hand and the lord of the manor on the other, because the latter claimed that his leases from the Bishop covered all commons in Gateshead. This dispute was finally resolved by the process of enclosure which has been described in chapter 4.

Municipal Corporations Act 1835

By the end of the eighteenth century, it was becoming increasingly clear that something needed to be done to replace these conflicting, overlapping and selfish vested interests with a more rational structure which could speak and act for the whole town, and the rapid growth in population which began in the early decades of the nineteenth century made this a matter of some urgency. In 1833, detailed proposals were put forward by a group which included W.H. Brockett, who later played a major role in the early years of the borough Council. This led to an enquiry conducted by two Commissioners.

The enquiry, held in late 1833, was opposed by both the borough-holders and the freemen. The borough-holders claimed that Gateshead was not a borough and the Commissioners were not therefore entitled to investigate it. They also claimed that the borough-holders were private individuals and their property was private property, initially refusing to open a box containing the borough records. When the box was finally opened, it was found that all the records prior to 1696, including any royal charter or similar document which might have proved that the town was in fact a borough, were missing, although the surviving documents did indicate that the town had been referred to as a borough for many years. In the event, the Commissioners reached a Solomon-like decision which had the effect of allowing the borough-holders to retain their claimed 'private property' while Gateshead became a municipal corporation under the 1835 Municipal Corporations Act, the passing of which happily coincided with their report.

Under the Act, Gateshead was divided into three wards each returning six members and with remarkable efficiency, particularly considering the time of year, the first election was held on 26 December 1835, the first meeting was held on 31 December and the second on 1 January. At this second meeting, George Hawks was elected to be Gateshead's first Mayor and William Kell, Town Clerk. Apart from the first meeting, which was held in a solicitor's office, the early meetings were held in the Anchorage despite a protest from

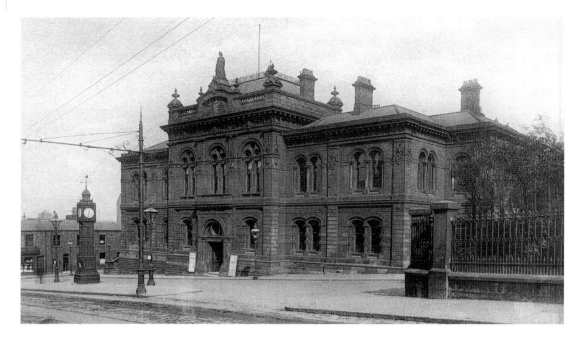

above The Town Hall built in 1870.

left The first Town Hall, in Oakwellgate.

opposite The unsuccessful Hillgate Quay.

representatives of the borough-holders. Thereafter, a house in Oakwellgate was used as a Town Hall until 1844 when it was replaced with one near the railway station. This had to be demolished in 1867 because of railway extensions and a purpose-built Town Hall was opened in 1870 and served until 1987, when it was replaced by the present Civic Centre.

1835 to 1974

Initially, the Council was dominated by industrialists led by W.H. Brockett and represented, for the time, fairly progressive views. During this period improvements were made in sanitary arrangements, with public baths and wash-houses being opened in Oakwellgate in 1854. One initiative, however, a proposal to create a Corporation Quay at Hillgate to offer some competition to Newcastle, seems to have been a complete disaster. The Great Fire and explosion which destroyed much of Hillgate in 1854 had one positive effect in that it cleared away many of the buildings which would have had to be demolished for the quay to be built, but the Admiralty insisted on a number of amendments to the original plans, the Public Works Loan Commissioners refused a loan, the North Eastern Railway was unco-operative as a potential customer and refused to improve the rail connections, and the unloading facilities were inadequate. In the event, it is not surprising that the quay did not attract much custom and remained a white elephant for many years.

Possibly as a result of this affair, a Ratepayers Association was formed in 1858 by what is often referred to as the 'shopocracy', the shopkeepers and owners of small businesses, who gradually took control of the Council and remained in power until after the First World War. The main objective of these men was to keep the rates as low as possible, with the result that Gateshead continued to lack many facilities which a more enlightened Council would have provided.

Towards the end of the nineteenth century, the Labour movement began to contest elections, but it was not until 1923 that the Labour Party finally gained a majority on the Council, following which Thomas Peacock became the first Labour Mayor of Gateshead in 1924. Opposition councillors were originally

An interesting combination. The Labour Party campaigning from a former Midland Bank branch in 1971.

grouped together as Moderates, but the Moderates were later replaced by the Rent and Ratepayers Association. The main issue dividing the two sides remained the rates, with the Rent and Ratepayers opposed to rate increases whereas the Labour Party were prepared to increase the rates to pay for improved municipal services, in particular to help combat the unemployment which continued to plague the town.

chapter nine

Gateshead today

Local government reorganisation

As already indicated, in 1974 the then Conservative Government carried through a major reorganisation of local government. Part of this reorganisation involved the creation of new 'metropolitan counties' covering the six major conurbations centred around Birmingham, Leeds, Liverpool, Manchester, Newcastle upon Tyne and Sheffield. Each of these was divided in turn into lower tier 'metropolitan districts' consisting of amalgamations of former smaller Council areas. Existing local government functions were divided between the two tiers. In the North East, the reorganisation resulted in a new Tyne and Wear County Council and the five new district Councils of Gateshead, Newcastle, North Tyneside, South Tyneside and Sunderland.

The new Gateshead Council area comprised the former Gateshead County Borough, the Blaydon, Felling, Ryton and Whickham Urban Districts and Birtley from the former Stanley Urban District. This covered roughly the same area as the former Gateshead Poor Law Union. The new Gateshead Council of seventy-eight members (later reduced to sixty-six) applied for a Royal Charter and became the Gateshead Metropolitan Borough with the continued right to appoint a Mayor which the former county borough had held since 1835.

Politically, all the Councils which came together in the 'new' Gateshead had been Labour controlled so it is not surprising that in the first election following reorganisation the Labour Party secured a massive majority, winning seventy-one of the initial seventy-eight seats. At that time, the main Opposition party was the Conservative Party. Since then, the Labour Party has maintained control of the Council, albeit with smaller majorities, but the Conservatives now hold no seats at all on the Council, their role as Opposition party having been taken over by the Liberal Democrats.

In 1986, the Government abolished the metropolitan county councils with the result that metropolitan boroughs like Gateshead are now unitary 'all-purpose' authorities carrying out all local authority functions including

Economic Development, Education, Health and Social Services, Highways, Housing, Leisure Services, Libraries and Planning. Initially, these were delivered through a traditional committee system, but this has recently been replaced by a 'Cabinet' system more akin to the House of Commons model.

The size of the 'new' borough was significantly larger than the 'old' one. The 'old' borough had a population of around 90,000 people which reorganisation more than doubled to around 200,000. The area covered increased even more substantially to a total of 55 square miles, with a river frontage along the Tyne of nearly 13 miles.

The nature of the borough also changed. The 'old' borough had comprised an almost completely urban environment, containing a mixture of industry and housing, much of it dating from the Victorian era, along with a number of areas of dereliction, but also including the giant Team Valley Trading Estate dating from 1936. While some of the 'new' areas incorporated into the new metropolitan borough followed a similar pattern, other areas, particularly in the west, were predominantly rural and agricultural with some residential suburbs but little or no industry.

Significant developments in the new borough

The new Council began a vigorous policy of investment in new and improved housing, business and leisure facilities, and the removal of remaining areas of dereliction to create a modern borough to which people and businesses would be attracted as a place to live, work and play.

An early policy was to publicise the town as a leader in the field of sport and recreation. As already mentioned, the development of Gateshead International Stadium as one of the country's leading athletics venues was given a dramatic early boost when Brendan Foster, the town's Sport and Recreation Manager, broke the 3,000-metre world record on the new running track in 1974. Since then the stadium has continued to host many national and international sporting occasions but has also continued to provide facilities for the local community, especially schools.

In 1986, an Art in Public Places programme began under which public and private sectors worked in collaboration to place large-scale sculptures in public places. This programme culminated in 1998 with the erection of Antony Gormley's 'Angel of the North' at the southern entrance to the town. This sculpture has aroused enormous interest both nationally and internationally and has joined the famous Tyne Bridge as an instantly recognisable symbol of the North East. Also in 1986, the Metro Centre – Europe's largest indoor shopping centre – opened in the west of the borough and continues to attract millions of shoppers each year, many of them from overseas.

In 1987, Gateshead Town Hall, a Victorian building which had become suitable for little more than ceremonial functions, was replaced by a modern Civic Centre designed to be 'user-friendly' for the town's tax-payers and large enough to accommodate most of the Council's administrative staff. 1987 also saw the first visit of the Tall Ships Race which was repeated in 1993 and is due to return in 2005.

The town has also been an innovator in the horticultural field. The Council's Central Nursery is one of the most modern nurseries in the country and provides plants for the borough's parks, gardens and flower displays, which have won many awards at national flower shows and in the annual Britain in Bloom competitions. The nursery also serves as a centre for two of the North of England's most important flower shows which draw over 30,000 visitors into the borough each year. In addition, as described elsewhere, with the assistance of a Heritage Lottery grant, the Council is currently engaged on a five-year programme to restore Saltwell Park, one of the finest Victorian parks in the North of England.

In 1990, the Gateshead National Garden Festival ran for six months and drew over 3 million visitors to the borough to enjoy a magnificent summer celebration. The longer-term result has been the recovery of a large area of formerly derelict land for use for private housing. A major feature of the festival site were the Dunston staiths, dating from 1893 and a scheduled ancient monument. The staiths are believed to be the last ones still in existence and are the largest timber structure in Europe. Sadly, they were badly damaged by fire at the time of writing. In 1991, the borough, which was already twinned with St Etienne in France, signed a twinning agreement with the Japanese city Komatsu, reflecting the strong Japanese industrial presence in the borough, notably through Komatsu UK in Birtley.

The years from 2001 onwards have been dominated by the re-development of the Gateshead Quayside area.

In 2002, the Queen formally opened the Gateshead Millennium Bridge, the world's first tilting-mechanism bridge which has been compared with the blinking of the human eye. Funded by Gateshead Council and the Millennium Commission, it has been widely praised as one of the best inventions of 2001 and already rivals the Angel of the North as a symbol of Gateshead.

The same year saw the opening of the Baltic Centre for Contemporary Art. This has been developed in a former flour mill at the south end of the Millennium Bridge and is the largest international centre for contemporary art outside London.

Nearby, adjoining the Tyne Bridge and due to open in 2004, are two impressive new buildings – the new Hilton Hotel and the spectacular Sage Music Centre, which has already been designated as the permanent home of Northern Sinfonia. The £70 million Sage Centre has been funded by the largest Arts Lottery grant ever given outside London, and will house a 1,650-seat hall as well as a smaller hall, rehearsal room, recording studio and a music education centre.

The Gateshead Quays developments were a major feature of the joint bid with Newcastle to be nominated as 2008 European City of Culture, but, in the end, Liverpool was successful. Although this was a sad result for Tyneside, there were positive aspects. Gateshead Council has promised to continue its cultural development policies, and the fact that it was a joint bid augurs well for future relations between the two sides of the river.

chapter ten

Some notable people

It is important to emphasise the 'some' in the title of this chapter because there are many people who have played a significant role in the history of the borough who have had to be omitted for sheer lack of space. Gateshead has also been particularly fortunate in modern times in having had community leaders of vision who have turned what was once the 'dirty lane leading to Newcastle' into today's modern and go-ahead borough, but it is probably too soon to attempt a proper assessment of the contribution they have made. Finally, there are a number of people who have already been mentioned in the companion book to this, *Whickham History & Guide*, and seems inappropriate merely to repeat information already available in that publication, but cross-references are provided where appropriate.

With all those reservations, what follows is an account of some of Gateshead's most notable residents.

Thomas Bewick (1753-1828)

Thomas Bewick, the famous wood engraver, spent his life in Cherryburn to the west of Gateshead before coming to live in the town. The site of his house, in West Street, was occupied by Gateshead post office until its closure in 2003.

Bewick was apprenticed to Ralph Beilby (1744-1817) with whom he subsequently went into partnership. He illustrated a number of children's books in the early 1770s and produced engraved blocks for books of fables in 1779 and 1784, but he is best known for his illustrations of country life, notably in *The Chillingham Bull* which was published in 1789, *The General History of Quadrupeds* (1790) and *The History of British Birds* (1797 and 1804). In later years he produced illustrations for *Aesop's Fables* with the assistance of his son Robert Elliot Bewick (1788-1849) and pupils, and was working on a *History of British Fishes* at the time of his death.

After his death, Bewick's Swan was named in his honour, and in more recent times his former home in Cherryburn has been turned into a museum dedicated to his work.

One of Bewick's apprentices, Charlton Nesbitt (1775-1838), also achieved fame as a wood engraver, becoming a silver medallist of the Society of Arts. An outline of his life appears in *Whickham History & Guide*.

Thomas Bewick's house in West Street.

William Henry Brockett (1804-1867)

At the time of Brockett's birth in 1804, the population of Gateshead was under 9,000, and by the time of his death in 1867 it had reached something like five times that figure. Brockett's great achievement as the dominating figure in Gateshead politics of the early nineteenth century was to ensure that the town's status reflected that growth.

Brockett was born in Gateshead in 1804, the son of a court official, and by 1827 was established as a general commission agent in Newcastle, although he continued to live in the High Street, Gateshead. In politics, he was initially a radical associated with people like Charles Attwood (see *Whickham History & Guide*), but later worked in collaboration with the Earl of Durham to ensure that Gateshead obtained its first MP in 1832 and a democratically elected Town Council in 1835. He was one of the first councillors, becoming an alderman and then Mayor in 1839/40. Among his many services to the borough, he established the Gateshead Dispensary in 1832 and served as its secretary for some years; helped to establish the *Gateshead Observer* in 1837 and became its editor in 1860; became a Poor Law Guardian; served as a governor of several voluntary schools; and was largely responsible for Windmill Hills becoming the town's first public park in 1861.

His business life was less successful. Initially, he became general manager of the Newcastle Marine Insurance Company and a shipbroker, and moved to a larger house in King James's Street, Gateshead, but in 1853, under threat of bankruptcy, he was forced to resign as alderman, sell off many of his personal possessions and move to a smaller house in Catherine Terrace.

When he died in 1867 after a short illness, however, the *Newcastle Daily Chronicle* commented that 'it will be a long time before [Gateshead's] inhabitants [will] find a man so willing to spend and be spent in their cause'.

William Cotesworth (1668-1726)

William Cotesworth played an important role in the public and business life of Gateshead in the late seventeenth and early eighteenth centuries. He was born in 1668 or thereabouts to a farming family in Teesdale but at the age of fourteen was apprenticed to Robert Sutton, a tallow and corn chandler with premises in Bottle Bank, Gateshead. In 1689 he was admitted to membership of the Drapers' Company, began taking on apprentices himself the following year, and went into partnership with his master's son under the name Sutton and Cotesworth.

In 1699, Cotesworth married Hannah Ramsay, the daughter of a prominent Newcastle businessman who was primarily a goldsmith but also had interests in coal and lead mining, and it was this union which laid the foundations of Cotesworth's fortune.

In 1705 Cotesworth ended his partnership with Sutton and began trading independently. Although he continued his activities in the tallow trade, where the demand for candles both locally and in London remained high, he also dealt in a wide variety of other products, selling locally produced products such as lead, glass, salt and grindstones to London and the Continent, and bringing in flax, hemp and whalebone from the Scandinavian countries, Germany and Holland, wines from France and Spain, and hops, sugar and tobacco from London.

Cotesworth's main source of income, however, derived from the coal industry, not, at least initially, as a coal owner but from wayleaves for moving coal over land which he controlled. This resulted from the will of William Ramsey, who died in 1715, under which Cotesworth became, *inter alia*, lord of the manors of Gateshead and Whickham at a time when these comprised the most productive coalfield in the world, and acquired property interests scattered throughout County Durham and subsequently the Shipcote estate in Gateshead as well.

Although Cotesworth was involved in a famous confrontation between rival coal owners about wooden wagonways being built over Whickham Fell in which the then Lady Bowes took an active part, Cotesworth's usual tactics involved lawsuits rather than direct confrontation. Although he became a coal owner himself in later life, and was a moving spirit behind the formation of the Grand Allies, Cotesworth was not, as may be imagined, popular with other coal owners and Sir John Clavering on one occasion referred to him as 'Black Cotesworth' who was 'not an honest man, but a rogue and a black devil'. In

Coatsworth Road, named, but misspelled, after William Cotesworth.

1725 his own butler and gardener even attempted to poison him, but whether they were acting on their own initiatives or had been bribed by someone else, which seems more likely, was never resolved. In addition to receiving jail sentences it was decreed that the two servants 'shall each of them every year on the 10th of June during their respective imprisonments be whipt 10 times about the market cross and shall each of them stand 4 times within the pillary each year upon every quarter day, with the crime for which they so stand in the pillary writ upon their foreheads'.

Cotesworth died at the age of fifty-eight in 1726. As already mentioned, Coatsworth Road, albeit mis-spelled, is named after him.

Sir Joseph Cowen (1800-1873)

A painting of Sir Joseph Cowen.

There were two Joseph Cowens, a father and son. Both served in turn as MP for Newcastle upon Tyne, and both could probably best be described as Radicals, active in support of the weak against the strong.

The first Joseph was born at Greenside in 1800 and served his time as chain-maker at Sir Ambrose Crowley's iron works in Winlaton. In his early years he became interested in the reform movement and was an active member of 'Crowley's Crew', the militant supporters of reform. In October 1819 he was one of the leaders of the Winlaton contingent to the great protest demonstration held on Newcastle's Town Moor following the 'Peterloo' massacre of demonstrators in Manchester. He subsequently became honorary secretary of the Blacksmith's Friendly Society on its formation in 1826 and its President in 1834.

As well as pursuing reform he also became a successful businessman, commencing the manufacture of bricks in 1828, later diversifying into gas retorts, and subsequently winning prizes at international exhibitions for the quality of his products. Later, he erected gas works, the gas being used initially to serve his factory but later, in 1853, extended to the (then) village of Blaydon.

He also continued a career in public service, serving as a magistrate, as a member of the Gateshead Board of Guardians of which he was Chairman for thirteen years, as a member of the River Tyne Improvement Commission of which he was Chairman for twenty years, as a member (later alderman) of Newcastle Council and finally as Radical MP for Newcastle from 1865 until his death in 1873. He was knighted in 1872.

Joseph Cowen (1831-1900)

Sir Joseph's son, also Joseph, was born at Blaydon Burn in 1831 and followed in his father's footsteps, both in the family business and in public service. He was active in both the Chartist and co-operative movements, and campaigned for improved educational facilities through the establishment of Mechanics Institutes, Reading Rooms and Free Schools in all communities, and Free Libraries in large towns.

Locally he supported the Winlaton and Blaydon Mechanics Institute in which he served as a part-time teacher, but he also addressed many open-air meetings elsewhere in the region and in 1854 became Editor of the newly founded *Northern Tribune*. In 1858, he formed the Northern Reform League and is said to have visited every colliery village in Northumberland and Durham campaigning for reform. Later he became Chairman of the newly formed Northumbrian Education League. In 1859 he became proprietor of the *Newcastle Daily Chronicle* through which he supported the successful 'Nine Hours Movement' to reduce the length of the working day in 1873.

The younger Cowen's activities in support of democratic reform had given him an international reputation and the list of European statesmen and revolutionary leaders who stayed with him in Blaydon at various times included the great Italian leader Garibaldi (in whose honour a statue was erected at Summerhill in Blaydon), the Hungarian revolutionary leader Kossuth and the French socialist and historian Louis Blanc. He was also a close friend of the Italian reformers Orsini (who was made an honorary member of Blaydon Mechanics Institute) and Mazzini, and at times offered sanctuary in his home to Polish patriots and other victims of Tsarist oppression. His reputation was such that Friedrich Engels, Marx's friend and collaborator, hoped that he might lead a 'proletarian-radical' party.

In politics, Cowen was elected to Newcastle Council in 1862, becoming an alderman in 1877, and in 1874 was elected to his father's former seat in the House of Commons. He retired from both the Council and the House of Commons in 1886.

top Cowen's brickworks in Blaydon.

above Joseph Cowen, 1897.

Ruth Dodds (1890-1974)

Ruth Dodds was born in Low Fell, Gateshead and lived the whole of her life in Home House there. She came from a well-to-do family – Joseph Swan, the inventor, was a great-uncle – and devoted the whole of her life to public service. At the time of the First World War, she was active in the women's suffrage movement and family welfare work. She also collaborated with her sister Hope in the writing of a standard text, *The Pilgrimage of Grace,* about the risings against the dissolution of the monasteries.

At the end of the war, she joined the Labour Party, becoming the Editor of the *Gateshead Labour News* (later the *Gateshead Herald*) in 1925 and a Labour councillor in 1929, with a particular interest in the fields of mothers' and children's welfare. As a Quaker and hence a pacifist, Ruth resigned from the Labour Party and the Council in 1939 because of its support for the Second World War, and thereafter conducted her activities mainly through the Society of Friends, although she did later rejoin the Labour Party.

Ruth also wrote plays including *The Pitman's Pay*, based upon the life of Thomas Hepburn, the miners' leader, which were initially performed by the left-wing Progressive Players in Westfield Hall in Gateshead, and later all over the North East. When Westfield Hall was needed for other purposes, Ruth and her sisters Hope and Sylvia provided the finance for a new theatre which survives today as the (non-political) Little Theatre.

In 1966, she was made a Freeman of the Borough in recognition of her long record of public service.

George Hawks (1801-1863)

George Hawks, first Mayor of Gateshead.

George Hawks was one of Gateshead's first councillors and aldermen who had the distinction of being the first Mayor of Gateshead in 1835, and subsequently served two further terms as Mayor in 1848 and 1849. Hawks was the head of the local iron-manufacturing firm of that name (jokingly referred to in a local song as 'Haaks's men' who 'won the Battle of Watterloo'). A brief outline of the Hawks family history appeared in *Whickham History & Guide.*

Hawks was not an outstanding Mayor. A list of ten motions voted on up to the end of October 1836 shows that he abstained on seven, and was absent for two. Why he voted on the tenth is a mystery. An anonymous writer at the time said that he was 'fond of associating with dignitaries and infatuated for civic honours', not perhaps uncommon failings, but it also went on to say that he was 'indolent in fulfilling public duties and distrusted by both parties', more serious shortcomings in a public servant. As a parting shot the writer claimed that Hawks could 'recite a speech, if long written and short to deliver'.

Whatever his shortcomings in other ways, Hawks set the Mayoral style for the future in 1848 when he bought a red robe and cocked hat to wear, and three years later, in 1851, his wife led a committee of fifty ladies who presented the borough with a gold chain and badge of office. The chain and badge of office, together with robes in the same style, are still worn by the Mayor of Gateshead today.

After his death in 1863, a statue to his memory was erected on Windmill Hills.

Thomas Hepburn (1796-1864)

Thomas Hepburn has a prominent place in coal-mining history as the man who founded the first mineworkers' union in the north of England. He was a moderate man, a Wesleyan Methodist and lay preacher, and, unusually for the time, was able to read and write.

Conditions in coal-mining in the early nineteenth century were atrocious. The work was not only very dangerous before modern safety legislation, it also involved long hours of work and was very poorly paid. Conditions of work were also extremely onerous. Employment was based on the bonding system under which men were tied to one employer for a year, although with no guarantee of continuous, or even any, work, but facing sanctions for breach of contract which included arrest and imprisonment, blacklisting and transportation which employers were not slow to use. Another evil was the tommy-shop system under which men were paid in tokens which could only be used in company stores to buy goods at inflated prices.

Despite the absence of trade unions (which were illegal until 1824) most miners in the North East went on strike for better conditions in 1810. The strike was not successful. The miners were starved into submission after seven weeks, their leaders were arrested and their families evicted. In 1830, however, Thomas Hepburn established the first permanent union organisation, the Northern Union of Pitmen of Tyne and Wear, which became known as 'Hepburn's Union'.

On 5 April 1831 (bonding day) the miners, now led by Hepburn's Union, came out on strike. Although Hepburn advocated a non-violent approach, there were a number of violent confrontations throughout the counties of Northumberland and Durham. In May, there was a mass meeting at Black Fell in Gateshead which led to negotiations with Lord Londonderry, the leader of the mine owners. These were initially unsuccessful, but in June the mine owners capitulated and agreed a number of improvements, including the reduction of the working day for boys from sixteen to twelve hours.

On 5th April 1832, a second major strike began but on this occasion the mine owners were well prepared. They brought in thousands of strike-breakers from outside the region and evicted the miners from their homes to accommodate them, with the result that the strike petered out and the union remained seriously weakened for some years.

Thomas Hepburn was blacklisted and reduced to selling tea round the colliery villages – not very successfully as many mining families were too frightened to deal with him. Eventually he had to beg for work at Felling Colliery and was only employed on condition that he severed all connection

left Thomas Hepburn's headstone in Heworth churchyard.

right Colliery banner at a memorial service to Thomas Hepburn in 1983.

with the union. He devoted the rest of his life to educational work among the miners. He died in poverty in 1864 and is buried in St Mary's churchyard, Heworth under a headstone erected by 'the miners of Northumberland and Durham and other friends'.

A successful miners' union was finally formed in 1869 and the bonding system was finally abolished in 1872.

Sir Charles Algernon Parsons (1854-1931)

Sir Charles Parsons, the famous engineer and scientist, was the son of the third Earl of Rosse, the noted astronomer. He was born in London and was educated at Trinity College, Dublin and St John's College, Cambridge before training as an engineer. He later moved to Ryton, now part of Gateshead, where he lived in Elvaston Hall.

Parsons greatest achievement was the development of the high-speed steam turbine in 1884, and in 1889 he set up his own company which installed turbo-alternators in many power stations and continued to develop more sophisticated versions of the turbo-alternator. In 1897 he built the first turbine-driven steam ship, the *Turbinia*, having first tested a model on his garden pond in Ryton. This caused a sensation at the naval review in that year, leading to the adoption of the turbine by the Admiralty, the Cunard Steamship Company, and later by other shipping companies.

Parsons was also interested in optics, developing many different types of glass for optical purposes and building large reflecting telescopes and searchlight reflectors. He was awarded many honours, including the FRS in 1898, the KCB in 1911 and the Order of Merit in 1927.

James Renforth (1842-1871)

In the nineteenth century, rowing on the Tyne was as big a spectator sport as soccer is today and was dominated in the middle years of the century by a series of three great oarsmen.

The first great champion was Harry Clasper (1812-1870) who was born in Dunston and was revered not only as a champion solo oarsman but as the head of a family rowing team as well as a boatbuilder and coach. A short account of his life appears in the companion volume *Whickham History & Guide*.

Clasper was succeeded as champion by a Newcastle man, Robert Chambers (1831-1868), who became the undisputed champion of the Tyne, Thames, England and eventually the world.

After Chambers' early death from tuberculosis, the championship passed into the hands of James Renforth. Renforth came from a Gateshead family although there is some evidence that he himself was actually born in Newcastle. He apparently started work as a smith's striker, which was an arduous and poorly paid job, and by 1863 he was married with a daughter and in urgent need of a more lucrative source of income. This led him, by 1866, to begin a career in professional rowing.

In this line of work the prize money was relatively low, the big money being made from gambling. Unfortunately for Renforth, he was so successful from the beginning that his supporters had difficulty in finding anyone to bet against him. In 1868, after a meeting in the Thames Regatta, the local champion, Harry Kelley, was forced to take Renforth on over the Putney to Mortlake course. Renforth was an easy winner which made his search for competitors even more difficult.

In 1870 a Tyne four visited Canada to accept a challenge from a crew from St John's, New Brunswick, and won easily. The following year they accepted another challenge from Canada and it was during this race that Renforth collapsed and died. The cause of his death remains something of a mystery. Renforth's body was returned to Tyneside and buried in St Edmund's cemetery, Gateshead amid widespread crowds of mourners. His funeral monument now stands outside the Shipley Art Gallery and a memorial stone remains in place at the west end of St Mary's Church.

George Ridley (1835-1864)

'The Blaydon Races', popularly known as the 'Geordie national anthem' and possibly one of the best-known songs in the world, was composed by a man who was born in obscurity, became a songwriter only when he was unable to work at a labouring job, and acquired local fame for only five years before meeting an early death.

George Ridley was born in Gateshead in 1835, the son of a rope-maker, and began work as a trapper boy at Oakwellgate at the age of eight. Two years later, aged ten, he moved to the Goose Pit in Felling where he remained for ten years. In 1855, aged twenty, he became a wagon-rider at the Gateshead Ironworks of

Hawks, Crawshay. Three years later, he was involved in a serious accident when a set of wagons broke away, and his leg was damaged so badly that he was unable to return to physical work.

While recuperating from this accident, he began writing song lyrics, and became a music-hall performer of popular songs. He published his songs in the form of a penny song-book on the back of which he described himself as 'George Ridley, Gateshead Poet and Vocalist. The most successful delineator of the day of local, Irish, comic, and sentimental songs' and announced himself 'at liberty to attend all meetings of a social character, and sing, amongst others, his own celebrated songs'.

Apart from 'The Blaydon Races', Ridley's best-known song is probably his last work, 'Cushie Butterfield', which named people he actually knew and who were, in some cases, not at all pleased at the way they were depicted.

When he died, in 1864, the fact passed unnoticed in the local press, and he was buried in St Edmund's cemetery in an unmarked grave.

Joseph Wilson Swan (1828-1914)

Although a Gateshead resident (at Underhill in Kells Lane) during many of his most productive years, Joseph Swan, the great inventor, was actually born in Sunderland in 1828. As a child he seems to have been a poor scholar, although showing evidence of an active and inquiring mind. After some years at a 'dame school', he moved on, at the age of ten, to a larger school established in Hylton Castle in Sunderland, and it was there that his scientific bent was first noticed. At the age of fourteen, he left school to become apprenticed to a Sunderland firm of chemists, but the two partners who owned the firm unfortunately died within the first three years of Swan's apprenticeship, which led to him joining John Mawson, the proprietor of a chemist's business in Newcastle, and moving to Tyneside. One eventual outcome of this move was the formation of the well-known firm of Mawson, Swan and Morgan.

Swan's first developments were in the new field of photography, where the existing chemistry-based technology was both cumbersome and messy. Long exposure times were needed and the quality of the finished product was fairly crude and tended to fade over time. Swan made a number of important contributions to the solution of these problems, most notably the development of bromide printing paper.

Although Swan's developments in the field of photography were undoubtedly important, his reputation depends mainly on his work in another new area of developing technology – electricity and its use for lighting. Many great scientists had been working in this field in the early years of the nineteenth century, including Sir Humphrey Davy and Michael Faraday, but it was Joseph Swan who finally managed to produce the first practical filament lamp. He demonstrated this to the Newcastle Literary and Philosophical Society in February 1879 and repeated the demonstration in Gateshead Town Hall in March of the same year. By the following year he had installed electric lighting in his home and his firm's shop in Mosley Street in Newcastle. Sir William Armstrong's house, Cragside, in Rothbury, was similarly illuminated by 1881.

In 1880, Swan discovered that Thomas Edison, the American inventor, had been working along similar lines to himself, although Edison did not demonstrate a successful lamp until October 1879. The two men agreed, however, that it would be sensible to co-operate, which led to the creation of the Edison and Swan Electric Light Company ('Ediswan').

The growth of the new business forced Swan to leave Tyneside in 1883 for the London area where he bought a house in Bromley in Kent, the first of several homes in the South East. He continued his experiments, however, developing improved filaments for his lamps and an electric safety lamp for use in mining. He was elected a Fellow of the Royal Society in 1894, and was knighted in 1904, but increasing ill-health eventually led to his death in 1914.

The Swinburne family

The Swinburne family has played an important part in the history of Gateshead for well over 100 years, with members serving in a variety of public roles but in particular as Town Clerks.

Thomas Swinburne, the 'founding father' of the family was born in 1795 and formed the partnership of Willis and Swinburne, attorneys at law, with his uncle Joseph Willis. Both partners played a prominent role in the public affairs of the borough and Thomas Swinburne was Clerk to the Commissioners, who functioned as a sort of Highways-cum-Watch Committee prior to the formation of the first Gateshead Town Council at the end of 1835. Amongst a number of other public offices he also served as Clerk to the Magistrates, who at that time sat every Saturday morning in the Goat Inn.

The first meeting of the new Town Council, which was held to select the first alderman, actually took place in the offices of Willis and Swinburne on 31 December 1835. The second meeting took place the following day in the Anchorage, the hall attached to St Mary's Church, and unanimously elected George Hawks to serve as Gateshead's first Mayor. The meeting also appointed the first Town Clerk, but there were two candidates for the post – Thomas Swinburne and William Kell – who each received nine votes, and the new Mayor used his casting vote to support William Kell. Thomas Swinburne thus narrowly missed the honour of being the borough's first Town Clerk.

In September 1856, however, Thomas Swinburne's son, Joseph Willis Swinburne, who had followed his father into the legal profession, was appointed to the post of Town Clerk following the resignation of George J. Kenmire, and held the post for over thirty-six years until his death in February 1893.

Joseph's son, William Swinburne, also a solicitor, had been appointed Deputy Town Clerk in 1891, and on his father's death was appointed to succeed him without the need for advertisement. He, in turn, held the post until ill health led to his retirement in October 1929. He died in the following December.

The two Swinburnes who served as Town Clerks held the position continuously for seventy-three years – a remarkable record of public service, which would presumably have been extended to three generations and a total service of ninety-three years if the Mayor had used his casting vote the other way in 1836, but even without this the family's record of service to the borough in other capacities can be said to extend well over a century. The family firm is still prominent in the Gateshead business world.

William Swinburne, Town Clerk from 1893 to 1929.

Robert Spence Watson (1837-1911)

Robert Spence Watson, the great Quaker and Liberal reformer, lived at Bensham Grove in Gateshead. He was educated in York and London before joining his father's legal practice in Newcastle, and thereafter devoted his life to public service. His main activities were in the political field, and he founded and served from 1874 to 1897 as first President of the Newcastle Liberal Association and subsequently as President of the National Liberal Foundation from 1890 to 1902.

Watson's involvement in political and social issues of the day, in particular his activities in support of peace and the freedom movement in India and elsewhere, attracted people from all over the world to Bensham Grove to seek his advice and assistance. He lent his support to many movements for reform and was particularly active in the educational field where his interests ranged from support for Gateshead Girls' High School, to helping to found the Durham College of Physical Science which evolved into Newcastle University. He was also Honorary Secretary of the Newcastle Literary and Philosophical Society for over thirty years from 1862 to 1893, and gained a wide reputation as an impartial arbitrator and conciliator in industrial disputes, for which he refused to charge fees.

Watson's physical energy was phenomenal. He travelled widely and undertook strenuous hiking and climbing holidays, becoming a member of the Alpine Club in 1862. Locally, he was a founder member of the Early Rising Association, the members of which met at 6.15 a.m. in summer months to take long walks, and also sponsored many sporting and athletic clubs.

Watson became a Privy Councillor in 1907 at the age of seventy but thereafter virtually withdrew from public affairs.

Konni Zilliacus (1894-1967)

Konni Zilliacus was probably the most charismatic and controversial MP ever to represent Gateshead, although he was not a native of Gateshead and his period as the town's MP between 1945 and 1950 occupied only five years out of an active political life. He was very much an international figure. His father was descended from Swedes who had settled in Finland, his mother was American of German-Scottish descent and Konni himself was born in Japan because, at the time, his father, who wished to see Finland freed from Russian control, was trying to escape the Tsarist police. It was probably this multinational background (the family also spent periods in Sweden and the USA) which influenced Konni's later interest in international affairs and contributed to his ability to speak eleven languages.

Zilliacus attended Bedales School in Hampshire from 1908 and from there went on to Yale. After graduating, he returned to Britain to enrol in the RAF and was naturalised in January 1918.

In the 1930s, he worked for the League of Nations and was a passionate anti-fascist, writing a large number of pamphlets under the pseudonym 'Vigilante'. He was elected to represent Gateshead in 1945 at the end of the Second World War but his opposition to the Labour Government's cold war policies led to his expulsion from the Labour Party as a fellow-traveller (i.e. a Communist sympathiser). The unfairness of this charge, and his genuine independence of mind, was illustrated, as Sidney Silverman MP pointed out, by his having the distinction of being refused visas to visit both the USA and the Soviet Union and of being expelled from the Labour Party all in the same year.

In 1950 he stood for Gateshead as an independent but was defeated. He was later readmitted to the Labour Party and was elected as MP for a Manchester seat in 1955.

Walking tour

Gateshead Millennium Bridge
and Tyne Bridge, 2004.

This walking tour covers the centre of Gateshead and begins in the quayside area of Gateshead, which is where the city's history began and where some of its most exciting modern developments are taking shape.

The explosion and Great Fire of 1854 destroyed much of the old property along the riverside, and in the twentieth century the building of the Tyne Bridge in 1927/28 and the slum clearances of the 1930s involved the demolition of even more old buildings so that there is little evidence left of the early history of Gateshead. There is still, however, much of interest dating from the town's growth in the Victorian era and subsequent modernisation in the twentieth and, increasingly, twenty-first centuries, with a considerable amount of interest being generated at the time of writing in connection with the redevelopment of the Gateshead Quays area.

The walk starts in the Gateshead Quays area at the south end of the Gateshead Millennium Bridge adjoining the Baltic Centre for Contemporary Art.

Baltic was a derelict 1940s grain warehouse on the riverside until 1992 when Gateshead Council conceived the idea of converting the building into an arts centre and obtained the backing of the Arts Council's National Lottery Fund. The building opened in 2002 and it is estimated that it will bring 400,000 visitors and £5 million per annum into the local economy. It is designed to be primarily a place for artists to work rather than merely an exhibition centre, and incorporates lecture and cinema facilities, a children's workshop, a library, bookshop and restaurants.

The Millennium Bridge is the result of another innovative decision by Gateshead Council. The bridge, which is designed for pedestrians and cyclists, first opened to the public in September 2001 prior to its official opening by

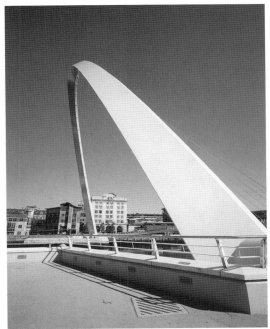

opposite The Baltic Centre for Contemporary Art.

top The Sage Music Centre, Gateshead. This innovative construction was completed during the summer of 2003.

above left Gateshead Millennium Bridge, 2004.

above right Bridges on the River Tyne, 2004.

the Queen in May 2002. It has attracted enormous national and international interest mainly because of its elegant and unique design which entails the whole structure acting like an opening and closing eyelid to allow the passage of ships beneath. The bridge links the redeveloped Newcastle riverside area with the Baltic Art and Sage Music Centres and proposed leisure complex on the Gateshead side of the river. From the bridge, spectacular views downriver and upriver towards the Tyne Bridge and other bridges can be obtained.

Walk westwards along South Shore Road, passing HMS *Calliope*, the Royal Navy Reserves base, on the right and the new housing and planned Baltic Quays Leisure Complex on the left, until the Sage Music Centre is reached on the left.

above Plaque on the Tyne Bridge tower commemorating the Great Fire of 1854.

opposite above Former River Police headquarters, now a club and restaurant.

opposite below *Tuxedo Princess*, the floating nightclub beside the Tyne Bridge.

The Sage Music Centre is a joint project between Gateshead Council, Northern Arts, Northern Sinfonia and Folkworks to provide a new home and touring base for Northern Sinfonia and Folkworks. It will incorporate a world-class concert hall with ancillary features including smaller/rehearsal halls, a music school and a music information centre. It is due to open in 2004/5.

Continue along South Shore Road which now becomes Hillgate, passing St Mary's Church on the left, and proceed under the Tyne Bridge approach road to join Bridge Street which takes you to the end of the Swing Bridge.

As you pass beneath the Tyne Bridge, note the plaque on the bridge tower commemorating the Great Fire of 1854 and the new Hilton Hotel on the left.

The Swing Bridge dates from 1876 and is the latest in a series of bridges which have occupied this site from Roman times. It is from this spot therefore that Gateshead may be said to have evolved over the last 2,000 years. The road called Hillgate which we have just passed along is the road running eastward along the riverbank and is one of the oldest roads in Gateshead. On the other side of the bridge approach is the equivalent road westward known as Pipewellgate, now being redeveloped as a leisure area. The first building on the right of Pipewellgate, now a club, used to be the headquarters of the River Police.

From the bridge itself, good views may be had both up and downriver. Upriver, the view takes in, first of all, the High Level Bridge and beyond that the Queen Elizabeth II (metro), King Edward (railway) and Redheugh Bridges. Downriver, the view under the Tyne Bridge takes in the *Tuxedo Princess* (the floating nightclub) to the right followed by St Mary's Church and the Music Centre with the Millennium Bridge and the Baltic Centre beyond.

Leave the bridge and retrace your steps along Bridge Street but bear to the right and then left up Cannon Street to one of the access gates into the churchyard surrounding St Mary's Church.

This former parish church of Gateshead now serves as a tourist information centre, but is of considerable interest in its own right as one of the oldest surviving buildings in Gateshead. Aspects of its long history are recounted in chapter 6.

From the church, return to Bridge Street and turn up Bottle Bank on the west side of the Tyne Bridge approach road.

Bottle Bank is one of the oldest streets in Gateshead and was not only the main street in the Middle Ages (probably the northern end of the Roman road from the south) but also the only road giving access to the original, and only, bridge across the Tyne. Sadly the construction of the modern Tyne Bridge and more recently the construction of the Newcastle/Gateshead Hilton Hotel have meant that nothing is left of the original buildings. One of the buildings which has disappeared is the Goat Inn, which was not only a public house but housed the local court and jail as well, so that it was said that a man could get drunk, be charged with being drunk and disorderly, be tried and then imprisoned, all without leaving the building!

At the top of the Bank turn right along Half Moon Lane.

The name of this lane is derived from the Half Moon Inn which stood at the junction with the High Street, but at various times it was known as Bailey (meaning Bailiff) Chare, presumably reflecting some link with the 'four and twenty' who governed Gateshead from St Mary's Church, and Marble Street because of Isaac Jobling, a sculptor and mason, who occupied a site there. At other times, one of the town's main wells stood here as did an early post office.

At the end of Half Moon Lane, turn left, cross the dual carriageway at the traffic lights and then turn right along Swinburne Street.

Swinburne Street was probably named after the Swinburne family of solicitors who provided Town Clerks for Gateshead for many years. The northern side of this street was demolished to permit the construction of the dual carriageway, but the remaining buildings on the south side, which still present a classical Victorian frontage to the world, at one time housed a number of Council departments including the original library, opened in 1885, which was replaced by the present Central Library in 1926.

At the end of Swinburne Street is the Town Hall. It was opened in 1870 following an 1868 foundation stone-laying ceremony notable for a fatal accident which occurred when a stand for spectators collapsed. It continued in use, although increasingly inadequate for other than ceremonial purposes until it was replaced by the present Civic Centre in 1974.

The clock in front of the Town Hall is an exact replica of one at Victoria Station in London with a 'Big Ben'-type movement. It was paid for by a former

opposite The Goat Inn, Bottle Bank, *c.*1910.

above Old Town Hall.

left Post office on the site of Thomas Bewick's house.

Mayor of Gateshead, Walter Willson, the founder of the chain of Walter Willson stores.

Immediately beyond the Town Hall is the Gateshead Dispensary, opened in 1855 to replace an earlier building built to deal with repeated outbreaks of cholera in the area from 1832 onwards. There is a plaque recording this on the side of the building facing Nelson Street.

A short distance past Nelson Street is the former Gateshead post office, which stands on the site of the house occupied by Thomas Bewick for the last eighteen years of his life. In Bewick's time, the site was an open one with views to the west as far, it was said, as the steeple of Ryton Church. Interesting features of the present building are the foot- and hand-holds which enable the police to inspect the inside of the post office.

Continue up West Street.

West Street was originally known as the Back Lane behind High Street, but it has had many names over the centuries, including King's Way, Dark Lane and Laing's Loaning. The large Tesco car park on the left was built on the site of Shepherd's, at one time Gateshead's leading department store. The nearby drinking fountain was erected to the memory of the wife of Sir John Maccoy, a shipowner who was Mayor of Gateshead eight times between 1912 and 1923, more than any Mayor of Gateshead before or since.

On the opposite (right-hand) side of the road is a statue representing Gateshead's sporting achievements, behind which is the Interchange Centre containing the central bus station and shops at ground level with Gateshead's main metro station below. Beyond the Interchange Centre are some of Gateshead's few remaining high-rise blocks of flats. This area is known as Barns Close and seems to have had a fairly lugubrious past. To begin with, the name does not apparently reflect the existence of any barns in the vicinity, but is a corruption of Burying Close, possibly commemorating a medieval plague pit. This did not prevent the subsequent opening of a quarry on the site which was later used in turn for the disposal of town refuse. Large houses were built on the site in the 1830s but these rapidly deteriorated into tenements which were severely over-crowded and, like other parts of old Gateshead, were badly affected by the cholera outbreaks of the nineteenth century.

Turn left along Ellison Street.

On the right-hand side of Ellison Street, behind the shops, is Gateshead multi-storey car park, famous for scenes in the film *Get Carter*, notably the one where Carter (played by Michael Caine) throws another character from the top level. Interestingly, the possibility of developing a restaurant on this level, which is supposed to be under discussion in the film, reflects the original real-life intention for this level which was never pursued for some reason. Most residents seem to regard the whole structure as an eyesore which it is hoped will be demolished in the near future.

On the left-hand side beyond the car park, at the junction with High Street, is a Tesco store, which was built on the site of the first Wesleyan chapel in Gateshead. This was the chapel associated with the story recounted in chapter six about the minister who attracted a large congregation by promising a fight – which proved to be one with the Devil.

Turn right up the High Street.

The area to the east of the High Street was the Bishop of Durham's park, a favourite area of his for hunting and the largest of the great landed estates which surrounded Gateshead in the past. The park is commemorated in the names of Park Lane and Park Road, parts of the Felling bypass which now runs through the area. It was in this area that William Cotesworth built Park House, which was subsequently incorporated into Clarke Chapman's Victoria Works before being destroyed by fire in 1997.

On the left-hand side of the High Street is Holy Trinity Church which was founded in 1248 as the Hospital of St Edmund and St Cuthbert. It fell into disuse after the Reformation and eventually passed into the hands of the Ellison family. The ruins were handed over to the Rector of Gateshead by Cuthbert Ellison in 1836, rebuilt and enlarged by public subscription and reopened as Holy Trinity in 1837. It was refurbished by Gateshead Council and now functions as a community centre.

A stone cross which formerly stood outside the church was the site of the execution of John Ingram, a Catholic priest, in 1594.

To the right of Holy Trinity is a doorway which is all that remains of Gateshead House, an Elizabethan house which was destroyed by fire in 1746 as the result of a slightly bizarre series of events. At that time Gateshead House belonged to the Claverings, a local Catholic family, and was used as a centre for Jesuit missions. During a visit to the town by the Duke of Cumberland, the victor at the Battle of Culloden, a number of people climbed on the walls to get a better view, but the gardener set his dog on them to which the crowd responded by setting fire to the house.

On the right-hand side, the Metropole Theatre used to stand at the junction of the High Street and Jackson Street. It was opened in 1896 and was by far the largest theatre in Gateshead, seating 2,500 people, but was converted into the Scala Cinema in 1919. The original doorway still exists but the rest of the building has been demolished with the exception of the adjoining Metropole public house.

Turn right up Jackson Street.

Originally, Jackson Street was known as Collier Chare, but the name seems to have been changed to Jackson Chare in the early eighteenth century, probably after Henry Jackson, a well-known estate steward to a local family, the Gerards.

After the junction with West Street, the line of Jackson Street continues on the far side as Walker Terrace, which was built in 1847 by a banker and shipowner called Walker and was one of the 'best' addresses in Gateshead, being occupied mainly by professional people. Before the construction of the Interchange Centre (which necessitated the demolition of the properties on the

The Civic Centre.

north side) and road realignment in recent years, this formed the eastern end of Bensham Road, the main road out of Gateshead to the west.

St Joseph's Church, which stands on the corner of Walker Terrace and West Street, was opened in 1859. It was largely financed by public subscription, working men paying one shilling (5p) per month. It was the only Roman Catholic church in Gateshead until Our Lady and St Wilfred's was built in Sunderland Road in 1904.

Turn left up High West Street and then right up Regent Terrace.

Regent Terrace was built in 1852 as a private venture, and was, if anything, even more select than Walker Terrace with gateposts and a lodge (Lambton Lodge), now an insurance office.

On the opposite side of the road, now a dual carriageway, stands Gateshead Civic Centre. This was built following local government reorganisation in 1974 and houses most of the staff needed to run the much-enlarged borough. It was officially opened by Neil Kinnock, the then leader of the Labour Party, in 1987.

This symbol of the new Gateshead seems to be an appropriate point to end this short tour of old Gateshead.

Further places to visit

The walking tour covers only the centre of Gateshead, but there are many other places of interest to visit in the borough.

Prince Consort Road

About half a mile to the south of the Civic Centre is a small group of buildings which reflect an earlier attempt to develop an administrative centre for the borough together with some more recent additions.

The Shipley Art Gallery and Museum was built in 1917 to house the art collection which had been presented to the town by Joseph Shipley, a local solicitor. Among the exhibits is a permanent exhibition devoted to Gateshead's industrial history.

The former Education Offices, now owned by the Jewish community, were opened in 1899 initially to house the Gateshead School Board. After the Board was wound up and its functions transferred to the local authority, the building was occupied by Gateshead Education Department until the department moved into the new Civic Centre in 1987.

The Gateshead Central Library was opened in 1926 to replace the original library in Swinburne Street when this became too small. The building has since been enlarged and now houses Caedmon Hall, available for public performances of various sorts, as well as additional library space and a small cafe.

Two more modern buildings are the former Finance Department offices, which now house the Gateshead Family Support Services, and the Gateshead Leisure Centre which accommodates a variety of indoor sporting activities.

Saltwell Park

Saltwell Park, which has been described in chapter seven, is arguably one of the largest and best Victorian parks in the north of England. It is currently being restored to its original appearance with the aid of a grant from the Heritage Lottery Fund and is well worth a visit.

Angel of the North

Gateshead Council has pursued a public art programme for a number of years but the best-known example of this policy is without doubt the Angel of the North, which was designed by the well-known sculptor Anthony Gormley and erected in 1998 on a prominent site alongside the A1 to the south of the central built-up area. It contains 200 tonnes of steel and is 20 metres tall with a wing-span of 54 metres.

Gibside estate

Further away from the central Gateshead area, the Gibside estate, ancestral home of the late Queen Mother, is also well worth a visit. The estate is now managed by the National Trust and contains a number of Grade I listed buildings including the Gibside Chapel, still used occasionally, the Banqueting House, which is available for rent for holiday purposes from the Landmark Trust, and the Column of Liberty. The remains of the original Gibside Hall, now sadly a ruin, are listed as Grade II. The grounds, originally landscaped in the eighteenth century, are criss-crossed by paths and riverside walks.

Angel of the North.

The Tanfield Railway in operation.

Tanfield and Bowes Railways

Two historic railway lines are still operated in the Gateshead area by groups of enthusiastic volunteers.

The Tanfield Railway was originally built in 1725 as a horse-drawn railway and the section still preserved may, in consequence, be the oldest surviving railway anywhere in the world. The line passes the Causey Arch, which is the oldest stone-built railway bridge in the world and is now classified as an Ancient Monument. Steam-drawn trains run on Sundays and Bank Holiday weekends throughout the year (except December) with additional opening on Thursdays and Saturdays in late July and August.

The Bowes Railway was designed by George Stephenson and opened in 1826 when it was one of the main colliery railway systems in the North of England. The line formerly included self-acting inclines and is open for special events throughout the year.

Bibliography

Ayris, I. and Linsley, S.M., *A guide to the Industrial Archaeology of Tyne & Wear*, Tyne and Wear Specialist Conservation Team, Newcastle upon Tyne City Council, 1994

Bennett, G., Clavering, E. and Rounding, A., *A Fighting Trade – Rail Transport in Tyne Coal 1600 – 1800*, Portcullis Press, Gateshead,1990

Bourn, William, *History of the Parish of Ryton,* The Wordsworth Press, Carlisle, 1896. Reprinted by Gateshead MBC, Portcullis, 1999

Bourn, William, *Whickham Parish: Its History, Antiquities and Industries*, G. and T. Coward, The Wordsworth Press, Carlisle, 1893. Reprinted by Gateshead MBC, Portcullis, 1999

Brazendale, Alan, *Old Gateshead*, Tempus Publishing Ltd, 2000

Brazendale, Alan, Various booklets and articles on the history of Whickham, Swalwell and Dunston. 1990 onwards

Brazendale, Alan, *Whickham History & Guide*, Tempus Publishing Ltd, 2001

Brazendale, Alan, *Whickham, Swalwell and Dunston*, Tempus Publishing Ltd, 1998. Reprinted 2000

Carlton, I.C., *A Short History of Gateshead*, Gateshead Corporation, 1974

Clasper, David, *Rowing: A way of life*, Portcullis Press, 2003

Clouth, Diane, *Joseph Swan 1828 – 1914*, Gateshead M.B.C., undated

Crystal, David, *The Cambridge Biographical Dictionary*, Cambridge University Press, 1994

Dodds, G.L., *Historic Sites of Northumberland & Newcastle upon Tyne*, Albion Press, 2000

Durham County Council, various information leaflets

Ermel, Trevor and Carnaffin, Eileen, *The Changing face of Gateshead*, Portcullis Press and Gateshead Council, 1992

Esther, Goff, *Requiem for Redheugh*, Gateshead MBC, 1984

Farrell, K. and Turnbull, L., *Windy Nook*, Gateshead MBC, 1993

Foster, Joan, *Our Bairns*, City of Newcastle upon Tyne,1997

Fraser, C.M. and Emsley, K., *Tyneside*, David & Charles, 1973

Gateshead County Borough, Official Guide, 1961

Gateshead Domesday Young Enterprise Board, *The Gateshead Domesday Book*, Gateshead MBC, 1986

Gateshead Herald and Post, various news items

Gateshead MBC, *Council News*, various dates

Gateshead MBC, *Official Guides*, 1974 onwards

Gateshead MBC, *The Gateshead Millennium Bridge*, 2001

Gateshead MBC, Various information leaflets and policy documents, 1999 onwards

Gladstone, D.T., *Made on Tyneside*, Portcullis Press and Gateshead MBC, 1998

Graham, Frank, *Famous Northern Battles*, Frank Graham, 1976

Harrison, F., *A History of Newcastle upon Tyne*, Hewitt & Rudge, Whitley Bay, 1912

Hewitt, J.M., *The Township of Heworth*, Portcullis Press, 1990

Lamb, J. and Warren, S., *The People's Store,* North Eastern Co-operative, 1990

Lewis, M.J.T., *Early Wooden Railways*, Routledge & Kegan Paul, 1970

Lomas, Richard, *Northumberland from Conquest to Civil War*, Tuckwell Press, undated.

Lumley, D., *The Story of Gateshead Town*, Northumberland Press Limited, 1932

Mackenzie, E. and Ross, M., *An Historical, Topographical and Descriptive View of the County Palatine of Durham*, Mackenzie and Dent, Newcastle upon Tyne, 1834

Manders, F.W.D., *A History of* Gateshead, Gateshead Corporation, 1973

Manders, F.W.D., *Cinemas of Gateshead*, Gateshead MBC, 1995

Manders, F.W.D., *Gateshead in Times Past*, Country Publications Limited, 1979

Manns, Ernest, *Carrying Coals to Dunston*, The Oakwood Press, Usk, 2000

Meadows, P. and Waterson, E., *Lost Houses of County Durham*, Jill Raines, 1993

Morrison, Keith, *Going Shopping*, Gateshead MBC, undated

Mountford, Colin, *The Bowes Railway*, Industrial Railway Society and Tyne & Wear Industrial Monuments Trust, 1966. Revised 1976

Nairn, George and Rand, Dorothy, *Birtley*, Tempus Publishing Ltd, 1997. Reprinted 2001

National Trust, various information leaflets

Nixon, P. and Dunlop, D., *Exploring Durham History*, The Breedon Books, Derby, undated

Oxberry, John, *The Swinburnes of Gateshead*, Robert Kelly Ltd, Gateshead, undated

Oxford University Press, *Concise Dictionary of National Biography*, New Edition, The Softback Preview, 1995

Portcullis Press and Gateshead Council, *Celebrating an Angel*, 1998

Rippon, Dorothy, *A Country Childhood at Ravensworth*, Parkdale Press Ltd, 2001

Rix, Thelma, *Whickham: 50 Years*, St Mary's RC Church, Whickham, 1998

Robinson, P.J. and Groundwater, K., *British Railways Past and Present: The North East*, Silver Link Publishing Ltd, 1987. Reprinted 1993

Rogers, Frank, *Gateshead – An Early Victorian Boom Town*, Priory Press, 1974

Shaw, Sue, *A Pictorial History (for the National Garden Festival)*, Gateshead MBC, 1990

Turnbull, Les, *Discovering your Neighbourhood*, Gateshead MBC, undated

Turnbull, Les, *History from Maps*, Gateshead MBC, undated

Turnbull, Les, *History from the Air*, Gateshead MBC, undated

Turnbull, Les, *King Coal*, Gateshead MBC, undated

Turnbull, Les, *The Tanfield Railway*, Gateshead MBC, undated

Turnbull, L. and Womack, S., *Home Sweet Home*, Gateshead MBC, undated

Winlaton and District Local History Society, *The Derwent Valley Walk*, Gateshead MBC, undated

Woodhouse, Robert, *Gateshead, a Pictorial History*, Phillimore & Company Ltd, Chichester, 1992

Index

Other local titles published by Tempus

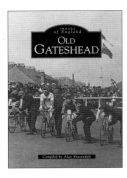

Old Gateshead
ALAN BRAZENDALE

This collection of 200 photographs of the old part of Gateshead captures the essence of the town in the late nineteenth and early twentieth centuries. This was a period of great expansion and change, during which the last vestiges of the area's rural past finally vanished and the great industries, which made the whole of Tyneside famous, reached their heyday. The pictures, many drawn from the collection held at Gateshead Library, show factories and warehouses, shops and private dwellings, schools and churches, transport and local people.
0 7524 2073 9

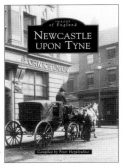

Newcastle upon Tyne
PETER HEPPLEWHITE

Selected from the Tyne and Wear Archives Service, this collection of 200 images portrays the city in a bygone age. The Tyne of course dominates the scene, new bridges are built and old ones demolished to cope with the changing demands of transport and industry. The quayside, redeveloped after the Great Fire of 1854, was a commercial centre of the Great Northern Coalfield. Leisure time was occupied in varied ways; sports such as rowing, bowling and curling were all enjoyed, along with football – 1955 being a golden year for Newcastle FC.
0 7524 1598 0

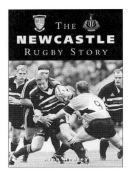

The Newcastle Rugby Story
ALAN HEDLEY

Rugby in the North East has a long, illustrious history and intertwined with it is the story of the Newcastle club, now know universally as the Falcons.

This book traces the 123-year story from the founding of Gosforth through to the great victories of the 1970s, when they won the John Player Cup twice in succession. Written by Alan Hedley, a rugby journalist based in Newcastle, *The Newcastle Rugby Story* contains many photographs and significant items of memorabilia from throughout the Newcastle club's history.
0 7524 2046 1

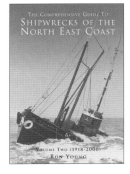

Shipwrecks of the North East Coast Volume Two (1918 – 2000)
RON YOUNG

In this second volume, from the last years of the Second World War to the end of the twentieth century, Ron Young charts the history of the ships, boats, submarines and their crews that were lost along the North East coast from Berwick-on-Tweed to Whitby, and the brave lifeboat crews that went to their aid, whatever the danger to themselves.

This comprehensive guide is an absorbing companion volume to *Shipwrecks of the North East Coast – Volume One (1740 – 1917)*
0 7524 1750 9

If you are interested in purchasing other books published by Tempus, or in case you have difficulty finding any Tempus books in your local bookshop, you can also place orders directly through our website

www.tempus-publishing.com

or from   **BOOKPOST**, Freepost, PO Box 29, Douglas, Isle of Man, IM99 1BQ
tel 01624 836000   email bookshop@enterprise.net